MARCIN GIERCZYK, EWA WOJTYNA, COLLEEN WILLARD-HOLT, EWA BIELSKA, DAGMARA DOBOSZ, MAGDALENA BEŁZA-GAJDZICA AND AGNIESZKA GROMKOWSKA-MELOSIK

# Supporting Twice-Exceptional Students in Higher Education

Connecting Theory and Practice for the Creation of Inclusive Learning Environments

NEW YORK AND LONDON

Designed cover image: Getty Images

First published 2026
by Routledge
605 Third Avenue, New York, NY 10158

and by Routledge
4 Park Square, Milton Park, Abingdon, Oxon, OX14 4RN

*Routledge is an imprint of the Taylor & Francis Group, an informa business*

© 2026 Marcin Gierczyk, Ewa Wojtyna, Colleen Willard-Holt, Ewa Bielska, Dagmara Dobosz, Magdalena Bełza-Gajdzica, Agnieszka Gromkowska-Melosik

The right of Marcin Gierczyk, Ewa Wojtyna, Colleen Willard-Holt, Ewa Bielska, Dagmara Dobosz, Magdalena Bełza-Gajdzica, Agnieszka Gromkowska-Melosik to be identified as authors of this work has been asserted in accordance with sections 77 and 78 of the Copyright, Designs and Patents Act 1988.

All rights reserved. No part of this book may be reprinted or reproduced or utilised in any form or by any electronic, mechanical, or other means, now known or hereafter invented, including photocopying and recording, or in any information storage or retrieval system, without permission in writing from the publishers.

*Trademark notice*: Product or corporate names may be trademarks or registered trademarks, and are used only for identification and explanation without intent to infringe.

ISBN: 978-1-032-94615-3 (hbk)
ISBN: 978-1-032-94614-6 (pbk)
ISBN: 978-1-003-57167-4 (ebk)

DOI: 10.4324/9781003571674

Typeset in Joanna MT
by Apex CoVantage, LLC

# Supporting Twice-Exceptional Students in Higher Education

This practical and action-oriented book focuses on addressing the educational needs of twice-exceptional students in higher education.

Drawing on the experiences of educators, this book discusses various challenges academic teachers face in meeting the needs of these students while presenting practical strategies that can be easily implemented in colleges and universities. Chapters not only provide a comprehensive overview of the latest research and findings in special and inclusive education, but also feature applications of the theoretical concepts and models discussed to provide interventions and techniques that can be used by educators and stakeholders in the education system.

Challenging the status quo and debunking myths surrounding twice-exceptionality, this book will pave the way for educators to implement effective educational strategies that uplift and empower these gifted and challenged learners within the higher education landscape and beyond.

**Marcin Gierczyk** is a Doctor of Social Sciences in Pedagogy and Associate Professor at the Institute of Pedagogy of the University of Silesia in Katowice, Poland. He is a crisis intervention specialist focusing on domestic violence and child protection. He is also an associate member of the McGill Centre for Research on Children and Families (CRCF) in Canada and an Honorary Research Fellow at the Jubilee Centre for Character and Virtues, School of Education, the University of Birmingham (UK).

**Ewa Wojtyna** is psychiatrist, psychologist, supervisor and cognitive-behavioural psychotherapist, and Head of the Psychiatry Department at the Institute of Medical Sciences at the University of Opole.

**Colleen Willard-Holt** has spent 30-plus years as a researcher, professor and consultant in the field of twice-exceptionalities. She holds degrees in both education of persons with disabilities and cognitive gifts.

**Ewa Bielska** is an Associate Professor at the Institute of Pedagogy, University of Silesia. Her research focuses on the issues of interdisciplinary perspectives of trauma studies and their application in educational research, as well as the issues of resistance theories.

**Dagmara Dobosz** holds a doctorate in Social Science. She works at the Pedagogy Institute of the University of Silesia in Katowice (Poland). She is the author of several dozen scientific publications. Her research interests revolve around the issues of gender, human sexuality, the sexualization of culture and the well-being of children and adolescents.

**Magdalena Bełza-Gajdzica** is a special educator and academic teacher at the University of Silesia. She researches the experiences of students with disabilities in higher education and promotes universal design. She co-develops national and international projects on special education and works as an expert for the Institute of Educational Research.

**Agnieszka Gromkowska-Melosik** serves on the Committee of Educational Sciences, Polish Academy of Sciences. She is a chair of the Department of Multicultural Education and Research on Social Inequalities at the Faculty of Educational Studies at Adam Mickiewicz University in Poznań and the Editor in Chief of the international *Journal of Gender and Power*. She is the author of 11 books, editor and co-editor of 13 books, and has written some 80 articles on sociology of education, contemporary problems of youth and multicultural society.

## Acknowledgements

We would like to express our sincere gratitude to the reviewers: Professor Sally Reis (Neag School of Education, USA), Dr Michelle Ronksley-Pavia (Griffith University, Australia), Professor Megan Foley Nicpon (The University of Iowa, USA) and Professor Garry Hornby (University of Plymouth, UK): distinguished experts in the fields of twice-exceptional students and special education.

# Contents

Foreword ix
The Gift Within the Paradox xi
Preface xiv

**One** — Understanding Giftedness and the Complexity of Twice-Exceptional Students — 1

**Two** — Students With Selected Disabilities – Implications for Work — 29

**Three** — Well-Being of Twice-Exceptional and Academically Gifted Students — 56

**Four** — Migrant Students in Higher Education – Chances and Obstacles to Successful Achievement — 78

**Five** — Blessed or Cursed? 2e Students Amidst the Meanders of Contemporary Mentality — 102

**Six** — Preparing Students With 2e for Success at University — 116

**Seven** — Conclusion — 144

Index 150

# Foreword

Despite growing attention on inclusion, higher education has too often overlooked students whose unique profiles fall outside traditional categories. This book brings into focus a group that has long remained at the margins of research, policy and practice: twice-exceptional (2e) students, individuals who demonstrate high potential, as well as exhibit one or more exceptionalities that impact their learning or development.

The increasing recognition of 2e learners, accompanied by greater sensitivity to their complexity and a growing academic interest, makes this book not only timely, but essential. It focuses on the educational paths and well-being of 2e students, emphasizing the importance of viewing them as whole individuals whose identities should develop with respect.

Written with clarity, depth and sensitivity, this book offers a compelling and respectful analysis of the challenges faced by 2e students in higher education. It challenges persistent myths in the field by offering a grounded, critical and nuanced portrayal of 2e learners. The book also serves as a guide for educational leaders and decision-makers who want to establish truly inclusive higher education institutions.

The inclusion of voices from psychiatry, psychology and education strengthens the book's practical resonance and cultural adaptability. It does not merely aim to inform but to stimulate reflection and drive action beyond basic compliance toward authentic institutional commitment.

The volume presents itself to readers with assurance that it will advance current discussions and initiate new research and institutional changes in the field. The academic community benefits from this timely and necessary publication because it creates opportunities for meaningful institutional transformation. Truly inclusive education demands both organizational dedication and collective discussions between multiple disciplines together with a mutual drive to reshape educational practices.

María Leonor Conejeros Solar
Pontificia Universidad Católica de Valparaíso
Viña del Mar, Chile
May 2025

# The Gift Within the Paradox

> The test of a first-rate intelligence is the ability to hold two opposed ideas in mind at the same time and still retain the ability to function.
> F. Scott Fitzgerald (*The Crack-Up*, 1936)

Fitzgerald's profound observation resonates deeply with the lived experience of twice-exceptional (2e) individuals, those who embody the paradox of being both gifted and challenged. These students possess high cognitive potential alongside learning, emotional, behavioural or neurological differences. They transcend conventional categories, presenting academic systems with a compelling contradiction: they are brilliant, yet vulnerable, capable of complex thought, yet in need of tailored support. In higher education, where autonomy, efficiency and standardization are often assumed, 2e students are frequently misunderstood or unrecognized. Many arrive at college with a history of misunderstood or overlooked learning differences. Others succeed academically but silently battle anxiety, executive dysfunction or social alienation. Their gifts may mask their challenges, and their challenges may obscure their gifts. A student may demonstrate exceptional analytical ability, yet struggle with sustained attention or executive functioning. Another may offer original insights in discussion, but experience acute anxiety that hinders participation. Such contradictions often leave 2e students caught in systemic blind spots, too capable to be "disabled", too vulnerable to be "gifted". They are forced to navigate institutions that rarely see them in full. The consequences of this binary thinking can be profound: unmet emotional needs, identity distortion, and a growing sense of disconnection from the very academic communities in which they long to belong. This binary lens, gifted or disabled, erodes the nuanced reality of twice-exceptionality. And yet, the very tension that defines 2e students is also a source of strength. It fosters creativity, metacognition, perseverance and divergent thinking. When understood holistically, 2e students are individuals with the potential to reshape the intellectual and cultural fabric of higher education. Their presence challenges us to ask: What does it mean to succeed? What counts as intelligence? How can we build environments that affirm both excellence and equity?

This book offers a timely and vital response to those questions. It brings together interdisciplinary voices, from education, psychology and psychiatry, to reframe our understanding of 2e students in higher education. Rooted in international perspectives, the book challenges educators and institutions to adopt a more inclusive, relational and developmentally responsive approach to diversity. Rather than treating exceptionality as a problem to be managed, it advocates for a systemic shift: from categorization to complexity, from compliance to compassion, and from fragmentation to wholeness.

The authors represented in this work illuminate the emotional, social, academic and institutional dynamics that shape the experiences of 2e students. They invite us to consider the risks of identity distortion when gifted students' emotional needs are unmet or their challenges dismissed. They reveal how institutional rigidity can suppress self-agency, leaving gifted minds entangled in self-doubt, impostor syndrome or quiet withdrawal. Most importantly, they offer pathways forward, practical, evidence-based and profoundly humane, so that educators, faculty and policy-makers can better support these students in realizing their full potential.

This book is a call to action! It equips its readers, whether they are lecturers, schoolteachers, administrators or researchers, to become agents of change. It invites them to question inherited norms, advocate for structural flexibility, and adopt practices that affirm the whole student. The book's international scope emphasizes the shared responsibility across cultures and systems to ensure that uniqueness is not treated as a barrier but as a valuable lens through which to reimagine educational excellence.

Let us approach this book not only as scholars or educators but as architects of possibility. Let us be open to imagining a university where students are not asked to choose between being gifted and being supported, where their complexity is not a liability but the very key to their flourishing. The twice-exceptional student is not a paradox to be solved, but a person to be known. The future of higher education depends on our willingness to recognize that contradiction is not failure but the seed of transformation.

Shirley Miedijensky<br>
Faculty of Graduate Studies<br>
Faculty of Education<br>
Oranim Academic College<br>
May 2025

# Preface

This monograph offers a multidimensional analysis of the education of twice-exceptional (2e) students within the context of higher education. While this topic has gained increasing visibility at the level of primary and secondary schooling, it remains significantly underexplored in university settings. The chapters presented here are the outcome of interdisciplinary reflection on the challenges faced by this specific group of students in higher education.

Twice-exceptional (2e) students combine exceptional cognitive abilities with cognitive, emotional, social or health-related difficulties. They need careful support, underpinned by research evidence, to address their complex needs. Inclusive support and student-centred pedagogy can help twice-exceptional university students overcome challenges, develop their strengths and successfully complete their university programmes (Kaufman, 2018). Understanding the importance of inclusive education and implementing effective educational strategies promotes the development of students' potential and skills, and facilitates their academic and professional careers.

Twice-exceptional students require well-informed, research-based support to address their complex and sometimes conflicting needs. While there is growing awareness of the needs of this population in some academic settings, this recognition is often superficial and not matched by the implementation of individualized adaptive support strategies (Jiménez-Soto et al., 2024). In particular, ongoing formative assessment, instruction tailored to their strengths, collaborative planning and social-emotional-behavioural supports are considered effective in addressing the multiple needs of this population.

Policies for supporting 2e university students include effective identification strategies and implementation of Gifted Individual Education Plans (Foley-Nicpon & Teriba, 2022). Universal screening would be ideal; however, in countries with large populations, it may be logistically or financially infeasible. In such contexts, empowering and educating parents to advocate for their twice-exceptional children during the admission process may offer a more practical and cost-effective initial approach, with formal assessments following as needed. Furthermore, there is a pressing need for in-service training for academic staff working with 2e students to ensure they are equipped with the knowledge and tools to foster inclusive and equitable learning environments (Kaufman, 2018).

Hence, this book will be of interest to educators, student support staff, academic advisors and university units such as deans of students offices, as well as to administrators involved in shaping institutional policies on inclusion and academic support. It is particularly relevant for faculties and schools of education, which can serve as key advocates and instructional design consultants for implementing inclusive practices within their institutions. In addition to its ambition to serve as a compendium of knowledge on the needs of twice-exceptional university students, the book aims to provide concrete recommendations and practical tools that can inform everyday educational activities. Its perspective, therefore, goes beyond theoretical discussion, offering applied strategies for creating supportive, inclusive academic environments.

From the theoretical perspective, we present important concepts in the education and support of twice-exceptional students. The authors relied on the latest international research in the field of special and inclusive education, as well as recent findings about twice-exceptional students and what services are typically offered for them at universities. Various theoretical models and their associated challenges and limitations are discussed. From the empirical perspective, we reference the well-being of 2e students compared to students without this designation. Action strategies, practical aspects of interventions and detailed techniques used by educators and stakeholders are described.

An important feature of the book is its interdisciplinarity. The authors come from different educational backgrounds and countries, and represent different scientific fields and disciplines: psychiatry, psychology and educational science. Among them are clinicians, researchers and practitioners who are academically engaged in the issues contained in this monograph. We are convinced that such a team of authors provides a multifaceted and innovative consideration of the issues. Emphasizing the importance of inclusive education in an international context, the authors advocate a global shift towards recognizing and supporting the potential of all students, regardless of their uniqueness. We encourage teachers and stakeholders to work together to create learning environments that embrace diversity and support the development of twice-expectational students within their own contexts.

By equipping readers with the tools and strategies to effectively support twice-exceptional students, the book has the potential to bring about long-term positive changes in higher education. It fosters the reconsideration of teaching practices, curriculum development and student support services. The book is intended to empower teachers and professors to become agents of change in their educational settings. It equips them with the knowledge and skills to advocate for and implement inclusive practices that benefit all students, especially those who are twice-exceptional.

Chapter 1 delves into the intricate world of twice-exceptional students in higher education, shedding light on the complexities of identifying and supporting these exceptional learners. By elucidating the definitions of gifted and talented students, it sets the stage for a deeper exploration of the concept of twice-exceptionality.

Chapter 2 explores the expectations placed on twice-exceptional students with disabilities as they enter higher education. It examines the challenges arising from their dual identity – as both students and individuals with disabilities – and the ways these roles intersect within academic environments. By analysing institutional expectations and recognizing hidden potential, the chapter highlights the importance of perceiving these students primarily through their academic role.

Chapter 3 presents the results of their research on the well-being of twice-exceptional students. In addition to a well-being index, two measures of giftedness in adults were used to substantiate giftedness, as well as academic achievements such as receiving a scholarship, authorship or co-authorship of scientific publications, participation in research projects or awards related to scientific activity.

While migrant students are not typically classified as twice-exceptional, Chapter 4 suggests that those who manage to succeed academically, despite the challenges of migration, exhibit qualities that resonate with the concept. Young migrants – especially refugees and asylum seekers – often navigate intense hardship, including trauma, displacement and structural obstacles within higher education systems. By framing socio-structural vulnerability as a form of exceptionality, the chapter expands the traditional understanding of twice-exceptionality and invites a more inclusive approach to defining student success.

Chapter 5 introduces the concept of the *right-thumb mentality* as a cultural metaphor that illustrates the societal pressure for optimization, efficiency and perfection – factors that directly influence how twice-exceptional individuals are perceived, diagnosed and supported. This metaphor provides an interpretive framework for understanding the contemporary challenges faced by 2e individuals.

Chapter 6 begins by summarizing pre-university experiences of students with 2e that either benefit or detract from their academic success, and then recounts ways that high schools can help them to prepare for university. Challenges posed by the transition to university are described, followed by recommended services for universities to provide. Strategies for success for individuals with 2e primarily include compensatory strategies. Descriptions of workshops for 2e students and for faculty/staff conclude the chapter.

Chapter 7 brings the entire monograph to a close by integrating the key findings from the preceding chapters, offering a concise summary of the main arguments and indicating directions for further actions and research.

The strength and distinguishing characteristic of this book are its focus on higher education in an international, interdisciplinary, yet practical, perspective, moving beyond theoretical considerations. As such, it broadens the discourse about 2e students in a future-oriented approach.

Authors
30 May 2025

**REFERENCES**

Jiménez-Soto, A., Infante Rejano, E. & Scurtu Tura, M. C. (2024). *No gifted adult left behind: Validation and reliability of the Adultgiftedness Identification Screening Test (AGIST)*. SSRN. https://doi.org/10.2139/ssrn.4988643

Foley-Nicpon, M. & Teriba, A. (2022). Policy considerations for twice-exceptional students. *Gifted Child Today*, 45(4), 212–219. https://doi.org/10.1177/10762175221110943

Kaufman, S. C. (Ed.) (2018). *Twice exceptional: Supporting and educating bright and creative students with learning difficulties*. Oxford University Press.

Understanding Giftedness and the Complexity
of Twice-Exceptional Students

# One

## INTRODUCTION

Despite extensive efforts by universities to increase graduation rates and students' academic success (Almukhambetova & Hernández-Torrano, 2021; Jacobs & Archie, 2008), support for the twice-exceptional population in higher education is still rarely addressed in research (Gierczyk & Hornby, 2021; McClurg et al., 2021; Reis et al., 2000; Snyder et al., 2020). Although most universities strive to attract talented applicants (Rinn, 2007), a lack of detailed research continues to exist on the adaptation of twice-exceptional students to the academic environment and the specific challenges of university-level work. This research gap highlights the need for a more in-depth understanding of the factors contributing to the success of this group of students. It is also troubling that, although a small group of students find success (Reis et al., 2022) identifying opportunities for their academic development, most degree programmes, at both the undergraduate and graduate level, fail to offer systemic support for talent development (Bazler et al., 2015).

Conducting research on twice-exceptional students who attend various types of universities is crucial, especially given the context of the assumption that talent development continues into adulthood (Gierczyk & Pfeiffer, 2021; Subotnik et al., 2011). The first year of university for twice-exceptional students can be a challenging period due to their unique characteristics and difficulties in adapting to new academic demands (Sandoval-Rodríguez & Conejeros-Solar, 2024).

## DEFINING GIFTEDNESS

### Historical Perspectives on Giftedness

No clear and universal definition exists of a "gifted" individual. Hundreds of definitions of the term "giftedness" have been offered, almost all of which refer to above-average development of a child in psychological spheres such as intelligence, creativity, and other non-intellectual areas (Renzulli, 2005). More common, however, is that these definitions refer to achievement and measurable academic performance (Hany, 1993). A variety of terms are used by researchers in this field, such as *high ability, gifts, capacity, abilities, aptitudes, skills, giftedness, talent, exceptional talent, prodigy, genius* and *twice-exceptional*. However, there is no clear consensus about defining the terms "being gifted" (Brady & Koshy, 2013) or "talented" (Gagné, 2015). This may be due to different research contexts, as giftedness can manifest in a variety of forms (Konstantopoulos et al., 2001), and its manifestation also depends on the support provided in the person's environment (Sternberg, 2003).

The concepts of giftedness and gifted students can be placed in the debate about objectivism and essentialism and social constructivism. Advocates of objectivism argue that it is a concept that can be clearly defined and measured with various types of tools, mainly psychological. Examination of the context of essentialism exists in the classic discussion of talent and giftedness focusing on an issue that has been discussed in psychology and sociology for centuries. Proponents of essentialism, such as David H. Feldman, believe that talent is biologically transmitted and, as he writes, "always possessed intrinsically" – as it cannot be acquired or learned. Proponents also include Howard Gardner, who sees talent as a form of "biopsychological potential", citing dance, chess or mathematical ability as examples. In this view, natural talent should emerge very early in life. Sidney Moon (2003) challenged traditional notions of giftedness grounded in fixed IQ scores, advocating for a constructivist perspective instead, defined as personal talent. Moon's work drew attention to gifted development's dynamic and multifaceted nature, shaped by personal needs, cultural influences and the surrounding educational environment.

In turn, Eysenck (1995, p. 15) points out that there are "genetically transmitted talents" that are "necessary but not sufficient for the emergence of genius". Without resolving the role of genetic factors, one can take a different approach and consider that ability – like love, patriotism or excellence – is a social construct. In such a view, ability is regarded as a relative concept, imbued with culture, social values and the power to define meanings. Borland (1997, p. 9) explains:

The construct has subsequently undergone many revisions, expansions, and redefinitions, but in one fundamental respect, until quite recently, it has changed very little. This aspect has to do with the belief, contrary to what I am arguing, that it is a thing, that it is "out there," that it is something that we discover in students. And because it is something in students, then students in whom it is found must be gifted. Thus, this construct has traditionally given rise to a qualitative existential dichotomy in which there are two distinct groups of humans: the gifted and the rest of humanity.

It is for this reason that psychologists, sociologists and educators working in the field of ability have struggled for many years to define the concept unambiguously. To understand an issue, it is not always necessary to comprehensively define it. If we cannot agree on a definition of intelligence, creativity or talent – which are the components of giftedness – we are even less likely to agree on giftedness itself. Cramond (2004) emphasizes that defining ability is a dynamic process. According to her, we should not define outstanding giftedness in an identical way in every country, because culture, language, art or the dominant religion differ according to the social context. Adopting a single, standardized definition would mean that the search for truth would cease, so any definition must be flexible enough to accommodate talents and abilities deemed valuable in each culture (Cramond, 2004). Moon (2006) also distinguishes between two types of definitions of ability: *conceptual*, based on theoretical concepts of ability that describe the characteristics of a gifted person, and *operational*, translating concepts of ability into the language of practice and providing information related to the process of diagnosing giftedness.

Cultural and Contextual Dimensions

Contemporary research on ability focuses on the psychology of individual differences. Throughout the 19th, 20th and 21st centuries, psychological constructs such as intelligence, creativity and motivation formed the basis for understanding ability. Defining giftedness and talent also varies according to the cultural environment in which it is analysed (Limont, 2010; Sternberg et al., 2010). One example of the intersections of talents and environment would be a culture without a formal education system, for example, where hunting skills may be considered a talent and the person possessing them would be considered as highly gifted (Fisher, 1998). Freeman (2005) notes that talent promotion and approaches vary according to the cultural and formal legal context of a country, leading to discrepancies in research findings. An individual's potential is more likely to be developed if his or her abilities are valued in a given culture (Gierczyk, 2019), and therefore society often decides what is considered a higher or lower level of aptitude (Balestrini & Stoeger, 2024).

A dual understanding of the issue is also common. A teacher, following stereotypical thinking, may consider a student to be gifted if he or she excels in knowledge in the classroom (Pfeiffer, 2015). A psychologist, on the other hand, may determine ability based on a high score on an aptitude or intelligence test. Currently, the importance of intelligence level for ability is not denied but is generally considered an insufficient indicator of outstanding ability. Environmental support and internal factors such as motivation, self-denial and creative thinking are also important (Raoof et al., 2024).

When defining *gifted* and *talented*, the Gagné model (Differentiated Model of Giftedness and Talent), distinguishing between "giftedness" and "talent", offers different perspectives (Gagné, 2005). According to this model, outstanding giftedness involves an above-average development of one of the natural human attributes, such as intellect. Talent, on the other hand, manifests through high performance in different areas of activity, e.g. in the arts, sports or science (Gierczyk & Dyrda, 2018). Freeman (2006) confirms this distinction, adding that giftedness is recognized in the context of intellectual development, while talent is identified by experts in the field.

### Theoretical Frameworks of Giftedness

When defining giftedness, one must consider the groundbreaking work resulting in the Three-Ring Conception of Giftedness by Joseph Renzulli (1978). Renzulli's work can be described as a theory that illustrates how the main dimensions of creative potential can be developed into creative productivity (Renzulli, 1984, p. 12). Renzulli conceived of giftedness as an interaction between three clusters: task commitment, above-average ability and creativity. According to Renzulli, each of these traits plays a significant role in the development of what he described as gifted behaviours. He defines above-average abilities as general aptitudes applicable across various domains or domain-specific skills in which an individual's accomplishments place them within the top 15–20% in that area. Task commitment, in Renzulli's view, is the energy one devotes to persisting with a given problem (task) or area of performance. The values most associated with this cluster of traits include perseverance, endurance, diligence, dedication, self-confidence and belief in one's ability to complete important work. The third cluster of traits characterizing a gifted individual is creativity. In defining creativity, Renzulli refers to a body of research identifying several dimensions of creativity across multiple fields. These include originality of thought and a fresh approach to problems, constructive imagination, the ability to go beyond established conventions and procedures when necessary, and the capacity to develop effective and original methods and solutions. Renzulli's work in defining giftedness is among the most cited work in the field.

### Developmental Models of Giftedness

In the relevant literature, there is a clear emphasis on the need to approach the concept of abilities from both theoretical and practical perspectives (Gierczyk, 2019). Particular importance is given to frameworks that not only define giftedness but also highlight opportunities for its development within educational settings. These perspectives underscore the role of key factors such as learning processes, individual engagement in specific domains and environments that stimulate growth. On this basis, three primary approaches to the education of gifted individuals can be distinguished. The first focuses on the characteristics of the individual – their personality traits, and cognitive, emotional and motivational dimensions. The second emphasizes the importance of support from significant others and institutions that foster development. The third highlights the influence of peers and the broader social environment in which gifted individuals function (Dyrda, 2012).

Erin Miller classifies contemporary conceptions of giftedness into two main categories (Mönks & Heller, 1994):

1. Descriptive and explanatory conceptions, which focus on the identification and education of gifted individuals. These include, among others, Gardner's Theory of Multiple Intelligences, Gagné's

Differentiated Model of Giftedness and Talent, and the Munich Model of Giftedness.
2. Formal (explicit) and informal (implicit) theories of giftedness, which differ in the degree to which they provide structured, systematic explanations of giftedness.

Formal theories have been validated through empirical research on abilities and intelligence. These include, among others: Renzulli's Three-Ring Conception of Giftedness, Mönks' Multifactor Model of Giftedness, Gardner's Theory of Multiple Intelligences, Sternberg's Triarchic Theory of Exceptional Abilities, Tannenbaum's model – the Talent Development Pyramid – and Gagné's Differentiated Model of Giftedness and Talent.

Informal theories, by contrast, are grounded in the authors' individual reflections and practical experience with gifted individuals. These are conceptual explanations of the nature of giftedness (Dyrda, 2012, p. 1).

Wiesława Limont, in her analysis of theories of giftedness, noted their multidimensional nature. Depending on the author, the concept of giftedness typically includes high intelligence, creativity, domain-specific aptitudes, motivation and a supportive environment – be it familial, peer-related or educational (Limont, 2008, pp. 13–14).

The author classifies existing theories of giftedness into the following categories (Limont, 2010, pp. 42–76):

1. Theories of general abilities
2. Theories of specific/special abilities
3. Systemic models
4. Developmental models

Theories of general abilities can be traced back to classical intelligence theories (e.g. those proposed by Galton, Binet, Stern and Claparède), in which giftedness is seen as a complex construct. These theories emphasize the significant influence of both internal and external environmental factors on talent development (Dyrda, 2012, p. 32).

Theories of specific abilities, on the other hand, differentiate between components of intelligence and variations in abilities within particular domains, disciplines or areas of individual activity. Examples include

Cattell's theory of fluid and crystallized intelligence and Gardner's theory of multiple intelligences (Dyrda, 2012, p. 32). Unlike general models, specific ability theories do not typically address personality or environmental factors; instead, they focus on the inter-relationships among specific components and their interactions with the environment (Limont, 2010, pp. 47–53).

Systemic models (such as those by Renzulli and Dąbrowski) conceptualize giftedness as a structure composed of interconnected, mutually influential components. These models prioritize internal conditions and view giftedness as a holistic structure of inter-related psychological processes and internal as well as external determinants (Dyrda, 2012, p. 32).

Developmental models (including those by Mönks, Tannenbaum and Gagné) emphasize the types and nature of changes that occur in individuals as a result of both internal and external factors. As Dyrda (2012, p. 31) notes, "developmental models, rooted in the paradigm of developmental psychology, describe changes in competencies over time as being influenced by both personal traits and environmental conditions".

Developmental models of giftedness, which constitute the so-called "fourth wave", emerged in response to the tendency of earlier theories to overemphasize the role of genetics in the realm of exceptional abilities. These developmental theories focus on the constantly evolving nature of giftedness and extend beyond the systemic solutions of the "third wave", taking into account a variety of external factors that interact with internal ones in shaping the behaviours of gifted individuals (Kaufman & Sternberg, 2008, p. 77).

### The Concept of Ability as Perceived by Gifted Students at University

One interesting study conducted by Gierczyk (2017) focused on the context of Polish and English gifted university students' understanding of the concept of giftedness. An analysis of various students' statements showed that they understood "giftedness" in three ways. These included the first interpretation, giftedness as dexterity, proficiency and speed leading to an intended result or outcome, i.e. "ability" equals "competence". The second way that giftedness was understood was as the ability to do something, i.e. "ability" equals "skill". And the third way was an understanding of giftedness as a high level of ability leading to an individual's outstanding achievement, i.e. "ability" equals "intelligence".

The students' statements included pictorial explanations of the concept of "ability", i.e. the so-called cognitive definitions, which, according to Bartminski, differ significantly from the lexicographical definitions. The data also suggests that the concept of "giftedness" is understood by Polish students in a manner that was almost identical to English students. Polish students defined "ability" by means of a connotative series, such as "creativity", "talent", "inclination towards something", "predisposition" and "organization of thinking". The view of the English students surveyed was that "ability" is an attribute independent of the individual – it is innate and natural. This is evidenced by the phrases "innate predisposition", "natural predisposition" and "natural inclination".

## SPHERES CHARACTERIZING GIFTED STUDENTS

From the point of view of the humanities, several spheres characterize gifted students, including the cognitive sphere (cognition), emotional sphere (emotion), motivational sphere (motivation), social sphere (social relations), physical sphere (activity) and character sphere (personality) (Heylighen, 1992; Tourreix et al., 2023; Vaivre-Douret, 2011)

### The Cognitive Sphere

According to this division, the cognitive sphere includes, among other things, original and unusual ideas, creativity, combining seemingly unrelated ideas, flexibility of mind, ease of problem-solving, high intelligence, vivid and rich imagination, speed of learning new things, excellent long-term memory, a wide vocabulary and a specific sense of humour (Asensio et al., 2023).

### The Emotional Sphere

The emotional sphere includes other characteristics, such as openness and sensitivity to the needs of others, low or high self-esteem, self-centredness, shyness, anxious behaviour, perfectionism and constant dissatisfaction with work outcomes, poor coping skills, anxiety and depression (Eren et al., 2018).

### The Motivational Sphere

The motivational sphere is characterized, among other things, by a tendency to seek information from a variety of sources, strong intrinsic motivation while relying on extrinsic motivation, frustration at tasks not matched to levels, a critical attitude towards the education system, clearly set goals, including long-term goals, and self-efficacy in arriving at solutions and acquiring knowledge (Raoof et al., 2024).

### The Social Sphere

The social sphere in the behaviour of gifted students can include a tendency to isolate themselves from their peer group (especially after being labelled "gifted"), poor group communication skills, an unwillingness to cooperate and collaborate (preferring to do things on their own rather than relying on others), attempts to dominate the group and a preference for the company of older people (Bain et al., 2006; Rocha et al., 2024). However, there are many gifted and talented students who are successful in interpersonal relationships (Eddles-Hirsch et al., 2012). Findings reported by Mahmut Çitil and Ufuk Özkubat (2020) indicate that gifted girls are more likely to exhibit advanced social skills, while gifted boys are more commonly linked to problematic behaviours. Additionally, this study demonstrated that gifted students exhibited significantly stronger social skills than their non-gifted peers, with this difference reaching statistical significance.

### The Sphere of Physical Activity

In the sphere of physical activity, gifted pupils may show, among other things, high enthusiasm and energy, continuous thinking, long concentration on an interesting topic, working to the point of exhaustion and spontaneity (Ferrándiz et al., 2025).

### The Character Sphere

The character sphere in the personality of the gifted individual includes, among other things, constructive non-conformism, a high sense of identity, a strongly integrated ego and high self-esteem (Popek, 2001). However, most scholars believe that gifted individuals are not a homogeneous group; rather, this is a diverse group in which each person is an individual developing at his or her own pace. Therefore, the characteristics discussed above may not appear in everyone.

## CHARACTERISTICS OF THE TWICE-EXCEPTIONAL POPULATION

### Defining Twice-Exceptionality

A twice-exceptional student, or one with DME (*dual or multiple exceptionality*), also known as GLD (*gifted learning disabled*), according to Assouline et al. (2006, p. 12): "is considered twice exceptional when he or she is identified as gifted/talented in one or more areas while also possessing a learning, emotional, physical, sensory, and/or developmental disability".

Other definitions have also emerged to describe individuals who display both gifts or talents and disabilities. The most cited operational definition of twice-exceptional (2e) learners is as follows:

> students who demonstrate the potential for high achievement or creative productivity in one or more domains such as math, science, technology, the social arts, the visual, spatial, or performing arts or other areas of human productivity AND who manifest one or more disabilities as defined by federal or state eligibility criteria (Reis et al., 2014, p. 222).

Students identified as twice-exceptional, in addition to having talents and high potential, also have disabilities, such as dyslexia, attention deficit hyperactivity disorder (ADHD) or autism spectrum disorder (ASD). The origin of the term *twice-exceptional* is often attributed to Elkind (1973), who introduced the term to describe students who are both outstanding and display learning difficulties.

### Terminology and Classification Challenges

The way we define learning disabilities varies significantly depending on geography. Confusion can come from when the term "specific learning disability" is shortened to "learning disability". While that might seem like a minor edit, it can lead to misunderstandings, especially when considering educational needs across different systems. In the United States, Canada and the UK, for instance, specific learning disability has a clear, technical meaning, usually referring to a noticeable gap between a student's intellectual abilities and their performance on standardized academic tests. This discrepancy is regarded as a distinct exceptionality, and students who meet the criteria are eligible to access specific support in schools. Things become more complex when we refer to students as twice-exceptional – those who are both gifted and have a disability. A student with Down syndrome, for example, would typically be described as having an intellectual disability. But in other situations, especially when referring to children with physical or motor challenges, the term developmental disability is used. This broader label can include conditions such as cerebral palsy and may help educators and specialists better understand the full range of a student's needs in addition to their cognitive abilities.

### Categories of Twice-Exceptionality

Twice-exceptionality includes students with above-average cognitive abilities, and those affected by developmental disabilities, various types of disorders and learning difficulties. These include, but are not limited to, sensorimotor disorders, autism spectrum disorder (ASD), attention deficit hyperactivity disorder (ADHD) and various cognitive disorders (Foley-Nicpon et al., 2013; Kranz et al., 2024; Madaus et al., 2023; Rizza & Morrison, 2007). However, children with chronic illnesses and cultural differences are not considered to be twice-exceptional. Being culturally or socioeconomically different is not an exceptionality but rather a situation that may depress scores on psychometric tests and, thus, lead to students being under-represented in gifted programmes. Also, those with chronic illnesses span the intelligence range and clearly require special attention within educational settings.

### Conceptual Models of Twice-Exceptionality

An interesting model of dual exceptionality was proposed by Ronksley-Pavia (2015). This model depicts the relationship between disability, socio-cultural environment and ability. Ronksley-Pavia (2015, p. 322), referring to Gagné's model of ability, argues for a comprehensive account of ability, and that:

> The features of this model highlight the developmental nature
> of giftedness, or potential for talent or achievement, rather than
> achievement being the focal point of giftedness. This model can
> contribute to our understanding of twice-exceptionality, in that it does

not define giftedness in a narrow sense of being only intellectually or academically based.

In her model, Ronksley-Pavia (2015) refers to *the social and cultural milieu surrounding individuals*, because, as she notes, the milieu in which twice-exceptional individuals live and learn determines the process of "categorization" of the individual and completes the characterization of children considered "normal" while belonging to any of the categories: disability, giftedness or twice-exceptionality (Ronksley-Pavia, 2015). As mentioned, the perception of gifted and talented is strongly influenced by the cultural and social context, since characteristics recognized as talents in one community may not have the same meaning in another. Ronksley-Pavia (2015, p. 334) highlights that "there needs to be societal and cultural shifts in acceptance of the coexistence of disability and giftedness and a shared understanding".

In many cases, in twice-exceptional individuals ability tends to be partially or entirely dominated by disability-related characteristics, which consequently contributes to the marginalization, stereotyping and exclusion of this group of students. It is important that their education takes place using models and strategies designed for gifted students, while also considering the working methods used for children with learning difficulties and multiple disabilities (Lee & Olenchak, 2015).

### Educational Approaches for Twice-Exceptional Students

Not all twice-exceptional children produce disappointing academic results. However, it is highly likely that, compared to gifted children who do not face similar difficulties, their abilities will be less well developed. Therefore, when working with twice-exceptional students, it is usually advisable to use what Renzulli and Reis have called the pedagogy of gifted education – that is, teaching methods based on strengths and interests that will fully absorb their attention. To enable twice-exceptional students to make adequate progress, the primary focus should be on building on their strengths (Renzulli & Reis, 1997). Since these students are not easily able to demonstrate their full potential and abilities, and their actual academic performance typically does

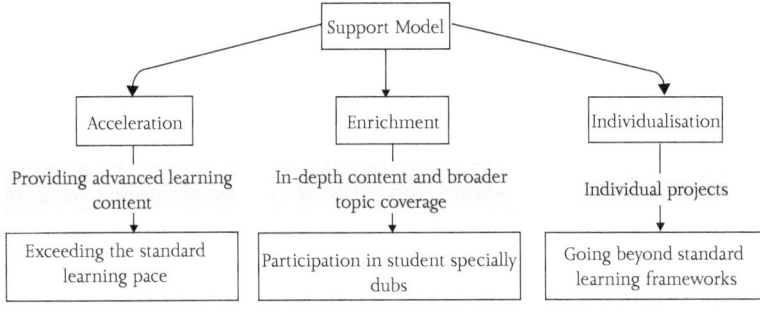

**Figure 1.1** Supporting students in acceleration, enrichment, and individualized learning

Individual projects could be implemented in any one of the three support models in this figure.

not fully reflect their capabilities, it is necessary to provide them with strengths-based learning opportunities as often as possible.

It is therefore crucial to ensure that they receive appropriate support and assistance in overcoming difficulties arising from their disabilities (Gierczyk, 2019). An interesting model of support (see Figure 1.1) is proposed in this regard by Eby and Smutny (1990), who distinguish three areas: *acceleration*, *enrichment* and *individualization*.

*Acceleration* involves the delivery of advanced learning content beyond the standard pace of learning. Enrichment involves in-depth content that includes a broader coverage of a topic; participation in interest-based enrichment opportunities and such things as student scientific clubs. *Individualization* means customizing learning to include the giftedness and the other exceptionality. Additionally, individual projects could be implemented in any one of the three support models in the diagram (Eby & Smutny, 1990).

## FACTS AND MYTHS ABOUT TWICE-EXCEPTIONAL (2E) STUDENTS

Many myths have emerged about *twice-exceptional students*, which often make it difficult to identify and support them properly. There continues to be a lack of public awareness about this group, often leading to misunderstandings in schools, as well as among parents and professionals. Below, we present two of the most frequently repeated myths and confront them with research findings.

### Myth 1: Giftedness and Learning Difficulties Cannot Coexist

The first myth is the belief that one cannot be gifted and have learning difficulties at the same time. This is well illustrated by a study conducted in Türkiye by Fırat and Bildiren (2022), which showed that out of 41 pre-service teachers, more than half believed that giftedness and learning difficulties cannot coexist in the same individual. In contrast, other research (Assouline et al., 2010) shows that 2e students are those who combine high intellectual potential with learning difficulties such as dyslexia, ADHD or ASDs. These two aspects can mask each other, with difficulties making the talent hard to notice, while talents can hide or mask learning difficulties. In fact, research shows that many 2e students are misclassified as students achieving as average and thus do not receive adequate support (Reis et al., 2014).

### Myth 2: High Intelligence Alone Is Enough to Manage Difficulties

There can also be a misconception that a student's talents automatically compensate for their difficulties. In thinking about both students without deficits and twice-exceptional students, there is often a myth that the intelligent child will "somehow" manage. This is one of the most repeated misconceptions. Many 2e students are left without adequate support because teachers and parents believe that their high intelligence will enable them to overcome any difficulties they encounter. These children often experience frustration and have lowered self-esteem because their difficulties are not recognized or are ignored (Assouline & Whiteman, 2011).

Supporting the view that talents don't automatically compensate for difficulties, Morin's (2018) analysis of support programmes offers valuable insights. Interesting implications for 2e student support programmes can be drawn from Morin's (2018) analysis. First, she points to the need to identify both the student's strengths and deficits because, contrary to popular belief, the former do not have a compensatory function. Second, it is worth noting that talent is not evenly distributed, and each ability may be accompanied by a deficit in another area. On the other hand, a study by Reider Lewis

(2021) noted that in teachers' statements, 2e students were simply described as "lazy", a pervasive finding also reported decades earlier (Reis et al., 1997). Seeing a student's shortcomings being due to their laziness or neglect is a mistake. It is important for educators and students themselves to acknowledge and accept these difficulties and focus on working in those areas where the student shows deficits.

The need to let go of preconceived notions when working with 2e students is critical. The perpetuation of myths – such as the belief that giftedness excludes the possibility of learning difficulties – often forces these students to mask either their abilities or their struggles in order to meet external expectations or avoid stigma.

### THE MASKING EFFECT

Masking refers to a situation in which a student's exceptional abilities and learning difficulties camouflage each other, making it difficult to identify them correctly (Lewandowski et al., 2006). As a result, twice-exceptional students are often unnoticed because their intellectual potential may overshadow or mask their learning difficulties; or, conversely, these difficulties may make it difficult for educators and parents to recognize their talents (King, 2022). This phenomenon challenges teachers and professionals who fail to see the full picture of a pupil's abilities and needs, resulting in misaligned or absence of support (Trail, 2022).

Many students with 2e function without adequate recognition, which negatively affects their academic performance and emotional well-being (Trail, 2022). Therefore, the importance of understanding the masking effect and addressing it in the diagnostic process is increasingly important. Only then can students be provided with an environment that will help them to fully develop their unique abilities and overcome the challenges they face (Maddocks, 2020).

Other research suggests that talent identification should go beyond standardized intelligence tests, as these can lead to erroneous conclusions and misclassification of students with difficulties such as ADHD or dyslexia (Atmaca & Baloğlu, 2022). The masking effect and limited educator awareness about this phenomenon may contribute to the lack of participation of twice-exceptional students with ASDs in gifted programming at university (Foley-Nicpon et al., 2020). This effect can also be an obstacle to their academic development, negatively impacting their performance (Yssel et al., 2020) and their support.

## CHALLENGES WITH 2E IDENTIFICATION

### Identification Barriers

The issue of identifying twice-exceptional students remains challenging, as there is no clear consensus in the literature on what this process should look like. As a result, the approaches used are often varied and inconsistent (Hodges et al., 2018), leading to misdiagnoses of these students (Maddocks, 2018; Webb et al., 2005). Webb et al. (2019, n.p.) cite the following example:

> Existential depression or learning disability, when present in gifted children or adults, requires a different approach because new dimensions are added by the giftedness component. Yet the giftedness component typically is overlooked due to the lack of training and understanding by health care professionals.

McClurg et al. (2021, p. 413) point out that: "The traditional diagnostic process is time-intensive, and because of the 'masking effect,' in which a student's area of giftedness or difficulty 'masks' their differential performance in other areas".

The same authors point out that there are three ways in which the masking effect, described earlier, hinders the identification of 2e individuals, which may consequently lead to a later diagnosis of 2e (see Figure 1.2). At the same time, they emphasize that: "Minority students are also unlikely to be identified as twice-exceptional" (p. 413). This is due to several systemic and social factors, such as the lack of culturally appropriate diagnostic tools, teacher stereotypes and institutional biases, which lead to the under-representation of these students in both gifted education programmes and special support systems (see chapter 4) (National Research Council, 2002).

### Conceptual Ambiguities in Identification

Additionally, the problem of identification may stem from the broadness and ambiguity of the concept. Knowledge of the psychosocial functioning of twice-exceptional students largely determines the effectiveness of their identification (Foley-Nicpon & Cederberg, 2021).

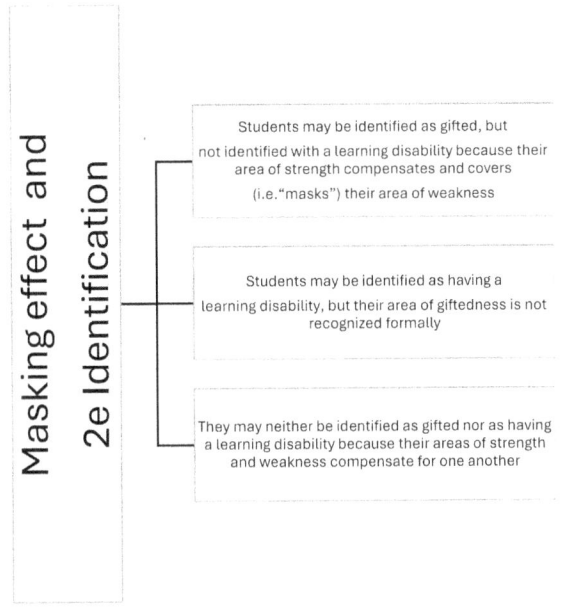

**Figure 1.2** The masking effect and the identification of twice-exceptional students

Therefore, when identifying a student's abilities, it is important to consider the fact that individual skill areas may develop at different levels and at different times. History notes many cases of geniuses in science or art who, in their youth, did not manifest the beginnings of their later talents, as illustrated in the following subsection. Because of this atypical development characteristic of gifted children, it is worthwhile to move beyond the generally accepted schemes for recognizing them and focus primarily on their educational, emotional and psychological development.

For example, Einstein, now recognized as one of the greatest physicists of the 20th century, did not stand out from his peers as a child – he reportedly began speaking at the age of 4 and writing at 7, and some sources suggest that he may have had a specific learning disability, such as dyslexia. Caruso, the Italian opera singer known as the "King of Tenors", was told by one of his teachers before he began his career that he should not sing because he did not have the right voice for it. By contrast, the mother of Edison, one of the world's most creative inventors, heard from a teacher that there was "something wrong" with her son's brain because he had an unusually large head; she educated him at home after his negative experiences in school.

### The Hidden Nature of Twice-Exceptionality

These examples show that not every person who, in retrospect, has been identified as gifted or talented develops in areas of human functioning better than average individuals. Giftedness and talent frequently remain hidden, and therefore the identification of twice-exceptional students, while valid, can lead to erroneous conclusions. Finding and properly supporting students identified as twice-exceptional is challenging, especially in academic settings. Their abilities and learning difficulties form an extremely complex picture that often does not fit into standard identification schemes. Unlike students who are clearly defined as being gifted or having learning difficulties, twice-exceptional students remain less visible in the educational system in elementary and secondary schools, as well as in universities (Foley-Nicpon & Teriba, 2022; Kranz et al., 2024).

### Recommended Identification Approaches

Successful identification of twice-exceptional students requires the use of a variety of diagnostic methods that go beyond traditional tests and include behavioural observation, contextual analyses as well as teacher and professional assessments (McCallum et al., 2021). This is pointed out by Coleman (2003, in Morrison & Rizza, 2007, p. 61) as requiring: "Nontraditional methods of identification that include questionnaires, self-concept scales, talent checklists, and interviews of adults directly associated with [the] student being assessed".

Due to the unique combination of high potential and simultaneous learning difficulties, the diagnosis of a twice-exceptional student cannot be based on a single indicator. Despite varying effectiveness, each identification method provides a good starting point for categorizing a particular student as a twice-exceptional student. The most common method of identification is an observation of the discrepancy between the student's performance, their apparent intellectual potential (IQ level) and the results they achieve during any kind of knowledge verification (Cao et al., 2017). However, this discrepancy alone is not sufficient evidence to classify a student as twice-exceptional (Dare & Nowicki, 2015).

Identification methods must also include the collection of subjective information using scales and measurement lists (Silverman, 2000), interviews and information gathered from members of the student's immediate environment – family, teachers or peers (Morrison & Rizza, 2007). As Crepeau-Hobson & Bianco (2011, p. 107) state, "create a balance between attention to the child's strengths and compensating for deficits".

## 2E STUDENTS AND HIGHER EDUCATION

As previously discussed, it should be important in identifying twice-exceptional students to apply procedures to identify these students in the pre-university selection procedure. Many 2e students are first identified for one exceptionality or the other at university level. This is the case because (in the USA and Canada, especially) recent psychological testing is required prior to students being eligible for any kind of accommodation (most often, they are given extra time on tests or access to a notetaker). In K–12 schools, educators do not test students regularly because of shortages of psychometricians and psychologists, resulting in high expenses and long wait times. Thus, it is necessary to create a list of criteria that indicate twice-exceptionality and apply them in the relevant questionnaires addressed to the candidates or in the observation sheets of those already admitted to the university. In most American universities, we find that students who are identified as having special education needs in K–12 (but are also very talented) don't always disclose their disabilities to their universities when they apply.

Some of the criteria that may support the early identification of 2e students include: a significant discrepancy between verbal and performance IQ (Reis et al., 2014), high academic potential coexisting with underachievement (Reis & McCoach, 2002) and asynchronous development between cognitive ability and social-emotional functioning (Foley-Nicpon, 2016). These criteria can be transformed into targeted indicators in the university admission process or orientation screening tools.

A practical example of implementation comes from the University of Iowa Belin-Blank Center, where specialized application forms and structured observation tools for faculty and advisors have been developed to identify potential 2e profiles. A similar approach is used in the Bridge the Gap Program at the University of Connecticut, where onboarding processes include self-assessment tools and psychoeducational interviews. Table 1.1 presents selected criteria and their potential applications in university admissions and student services.

Such diagnostic tools and support systems not only improve the accuracy of 2e student identification, but also foster a more inclusive and responsive academic environment. As Abunasser and AlAli (2022) emphasize, universities should adopt strengths-based, talent-focused approaches that address both giftedness and support needs.

It is also important in working with 2e students to create an environment that supports their talents by adapting their educational programmes for them. Such programmes are based on abstract thinking and creativity, which can increase the motivation of these students and reduce the level of frustration associated with deficits. It is also important here to focus assignments on the talents and interests of 2e students and their preferred learning styles (Bracamonte, 2010). Among students with twice-exceptionalities and learning

**Table 1.1** Criteria and applications in university admissions

| Criterion | Potential indicators | Application in higher education |
|---|---|---|
| Discrepancy between IQ and school performance | High standardized test scores (e.g. SAT, national exams) with low GPA | Analysis of admissions documents; flagging profiles with discrepancies |
| Creativity with difficulties in structured output | Strong visual or conceptual thinking; challenges in essay writing | Optional creative portfolios or multimedia formats during application |
| Perfectionism and anxiety masking difficulties | Student self-reports of stress, emotional withdrawal, poor adaptation | Brief well-being questionnaires during registration; early support sessions |
| Metacognitive strengths with executive function challenges | Strong conceptual planning; organizational difficulties | Faculty and advisor training to detect "invisible difficulties" |

disabilities (LDs) in higher education, there are differences in academic achievement in STEM disciplines (science, technology, engineering and mathematics).

## CONCLUSION

The concept of twice-exceptionality is a complex issue in both definition and identification contexts. An accurate diagnosis, supported by appropriate assistance, can contribute to improving the well-being of these students at elementary and secondary schools, as well as at the university level. Additionally, masking effects and asynchronous or uneven development can contribute to confusion of identification and complicate the selection and implementation of support and talent development strategies (Baum et al., 2014; Foley-Nicpon et al., 2013; Reis et al., 2014). Without this support, these students will not fully develop their abilities.

## REFERENCES

Abeysekera, I. (2014). Giftedness and talent in university education: A review of issues and perspectives. *Gifted and Talented International*, 29(1–2), 137–146.

Abunasser, F. & AlAli, R. (2022). Do faculty members apply the standards for developing gifted students at universities? An exploratory study. *European Journal of Investigation in Health, Psychology and Education*, 12(6), 579–600. https://doi.org/10.3390/ejihpe12060043

Acar, S., Sen, S. & Cayirdag, N. (2016). Consistency of the performance and non-performance methods in gifted identification: A multilevel meta-analytic review. *Gifted Child Quarterly*, 60(2).

Almukhambetova, A. & Hernández-Torrano, D. (2021). On being gifted at university: Academic, social, emotional, and institutional adjustment in Kazakhstan. *Journal of Advanced Academics*, 32(1), 70–91. https://doi.org/10.1177/1932202X20951825

Anderson, A. H., Carter, M. & Stephenson, J. (2017). Perspectives of university students with autism spectrum disorder. *Journal of Autism and Developmental Disorders*, 48(3), 651–665. https://doi.org/10.1007/s10803-017-3257-3

Asensio, D., Duñabeitia, J. A. & Fernández-Mera, A. (2023). The cognitive profile of intellectual giftedness. *International Journal of Educational Psychology*, July. https://doi.org/10.17583/ijep.11828

Assouline, S. G., Foley Nicpon, M. & Huber, D. H. (2006). The impact of vulnerabilities and strengths on the academic experiences of twice-exceptional students: A message to school counselors. *Professional School Counseling*, 10, 14–24.

Assouline, S. G., Foley Nicpon, M. & Whiteman, C. (2010). Cognitive and psychosocial characteristics of gifted students with written language disability. *Gifted Child Quarterly*, 54(2), 102–115. https://doi.org/10.1177/0016986209355974

Assouline, S. G. & Whiteman, C. S. (2011). Twice-exceptionality: Implications for school psychologists in the post-IDEA 2004 era. *Psychology in the Schools*, 48(8), 657–671.

Atmaca, F. & Baloğlu, M. (2022). The two sides of cognitive masking: A three-level Bayesian meta-analysis on twice-exceptionality. *Gifted Child Quarterly*, 66(4), 277–295.

Bain, S. K., Choate, S. M. & Bliss, S. L. (2006). Perceptions of developmental, social, and emotional issues in giftedness: Are they realistic? *Roeper Review*, 29(1), 41–48. https://doi.org/10.1080/02783190609554383

Balduf, M. (2009). Underachievement among college students. *Journal of Advanced Academics*, 20(2), 274–294. https://doi.org/10.1177/1932202X0902000204

Balestrini, D. P. & Stoeger, H. (2024). Cultural framing of giftedness in recent US fictional texts. *PLOS ONE*, 19(8), e0307222. https://doi.org/10.1371/journal.pone.0307222

Baum, S. & Owen, S. V. (1988). High ability/learning disabled students: How are they different? *Gifted Child Quarterly*, 32(3), 321–326. https://doi.org/10.1177/001698628803200305

Baum, S. M., Schader, R. M. & Hébert, T. P. (2014). Through a different lens: Reflecting on a strengths-based, talent-focused approach for twice-exceptional learners. *Gifted Child Quarterly*, 58(4), 311–327. https://doi.org/10.1177/0016986214547632

Bazler, J., Graybill, L. & Van Sickle, M. (2015). Historical overview of adult gifted education in the United States. In *Special and gifted education: Concepts, methodologies, tools, and applications*. MAIR.

Borland, J. H. (1997). Construct of giftedness. *Peabody Journal of Education*, 72(3/4), 6–20.

Bracamonte, M. (2010). Twice-exceptional students: Who they are and what they need. Davidson Institute for Talent Development. https://www.davidsongifted.org/gifted-blog/2e-students-who-they-are-and-what-they-need/ [accessed 1 January 2025]

Brady, M. & Koshy, V. (2013). Reflections on the implementation of the gifted and talented policy in England, 1999–2011. *Gifted Education International*, 30(3), 254–266.

Brown, P. & Tannock, S. (2009). Education, meritocracy and the global war for talent. *Journal of Education Policy*, 24(4).

Cao, T. H., Jung, J. Y. & Lee, J. (2017). Assessment in gifted education: A review of the literature from 2005 to 2016. *Journal of Advanced Academics*, 28(3), 163–203. https://doi.org/10.1177/1932202x17714572

Çitil, M. & Özkubat, U. (2020). The comparison of the social skills, problem behaviours and academic competence of gifted students and their non-gifted peers. *International Journal of Progressive Education*, 16(6), 1–14.

Coleman, M. R. (2003). *The identification of students who are gifted*. Arlington, VA: ERIC Clearinghouse on Disabilities and Gifted Education. (ERIC Service Reproduction No. ED480431)

Coleman, M. R., Harradine, C. & King, W. E. (2005). Meeting the needs of students who are twice exceptional. *Teaching Exceptional Children*, 38(1).

Cramond, B. (2004). Can we, should we, need we agree on a definition of giftedness? *Roeper Review*, 21(1), 15.

Crepeau-Hobson, F. & Bianco, M. (2011). Identification of gifted students with learning disabilities in a response-to-intervention era. *Psychology in the Schools*, 48(2), 102–109. https://doi.org/10.1002/pits.20528

Dare, L. & Nowicki, E. A. (2015). Twice-exceptionality: Parents' perspectives on 2e identification. *Roeper Review*, 37(4), 208–218. https://doi.org/10.1080/02783193.2015.1077911

Dyrda, B. (2012). *Edukacyjne wspieranie rozwoju uczniów zdolnych. Studium społeczno-pedagogiczne*. Wydawnictwo Żak.

Dyrda, B. & Gierczyk, M. K. (2013). Indywidualizacja pracy z uczniem uzdolnionym matematycznie: przykłady dobrej praktyki w szkolnictwie brytyjskim. In *Wczesnoszkolna edukacja matematyczna ograniczenia i ich przełamywanie* (pp. 183–191). Wydawnictwo Uniwersytetu Warmińsko-Mazurskiego.

Eby, J. W. & Smutny, J. F. (1990). *A thoughtful overview of gifted education*. Longman.

Eddles-Hirsch, K., Vialle, W., McCormick, J. & Rogers, K. (2012). Insiders or outsiders: The role of social context in the peer relations of gifted students. *Roeper Review*, 34, 53–62.

Elkind, J. (1973). The gifted child with learning disabilities. *Gifted Child Quarterly*, 17(3).

Eren, F., Çete, A. Ö., Avcil, S. & Baykara, B. (2018). Emotional and behavioral characteristics of gifted children and their families. *Noro Psikiyatri Arsivi*, 55(2), 105–112. https://doi.org/10.5152/npa.2017.12731

Eysenck, H. J. (1995). *Genius: the natural history of creativity*. Cambridge University Press.

Ferrándiz, C., Ferrando-Prieto, M., Infantes-Paniagua, Á., Fernández Vidal, M. C. & Pons, R. M. (2025). Pre-service teachers' perceptions of physical, socioemotional, and cognitive traits in gifted students: Unveiling bias? *Frontiers in Sports and Active Living*, 6, 1472880. https://doi.org/10.3389/fspor.2024.1472880

Fisher, R. (1998). *Teaching thinking: Philosophical enquiry in the classroom*. Continuum.

Fırat, T. & Bildiren, A. (2022). The characteristics of gifted children with learning disabilities according to preschool teachers. *Early Years*, 43(4–5), 921–937. https://doi.org/10.1080/09575146.2022.2034755

Foley-Nicpon, M. (2016). The social and emotional development of twice-exceptional children. In M. Neihart, S. I. Pfeiffer & T. L. Cross (Eds.), *The social and emotional development of gifted children* (2nd ed., pp. 103–118). Routledge. https://doi.org/10.4324/9781003238928

Foley-Nicpon, M., Assouline, S. G. & Coangelo, N. (2013). Twice-exceptional learners: Who needs to know what? *Gifted Child Quarterly*, 57(3), 169–180. https://doi.org/10.1177/0016986213490021

Foley-Nicpon, M. & Cederberg, C. (2021). Moving beyond disabilities: Twice-exceptional students and self-advocacy. In J. Lawson-Davis & D. Douglas (Eds.), *Empowering underrepresented gifted students: Perspectives from the field* (pp. 116–125). Free Spirit Publishing.

Foley-Nicpon, M., Cederberg, C. D. & Wienkes, C. (2020). Autism spectrum disorders and high ability. In J. Plucker & C. Callahan (Eds.), *Critical issues and practices in gifted education: A survey of current research on giftedness and talent development* (3rd ed., pp. 13–26). Routledge. https://doi.org/10.4324/9781003233961

Foley-Nicpon, M. & Lin, C. L. R. (2022). Identifying and providing instructional services for twice-exceptional students. In *Identifying and serving diverse gifted learners* (pp. 188–200). Routledge.

Foley-Nicpon, M. & Teriba, A. (2022). Policy considerations for twice-exceptional students. *Gifted Child Today*, 45(4), 212–219. https://doi.org/10.1177/10762175 221110943

Freeman, J. (2005). Permission to be gifted: How conceptions of giftedness can change lives. In R. Sternberg & J. Davidson (Eds.), *Conceptions of giftedness*. Cambridge University Press.

Freeman, J. (2006). The emotional development of gifted and talented children. *Gifted and Talented International*, 21(2), 20–28. https://doi.org/10.1080/15332276.2006. 11673472

Freeman, J. (2015). Cultural variations in ideas of gifts and talents with special regard to the Eastern and Western worlds. In D. Y. Dai & C. K. Ching (Eds.), *Gifted education in Asia* (pp. 231–244). Information Age Publishing.

Gagné, F. (2005). From gifts to talents: The DMGT as a developmental model. In R. J. Sternberg & J. E. Davidson (Eds.), *Conceptions of giftedness*. Cambridge University Press.

Gagné, F. (1991). Toward a differential model of giftedness and talent. In N. Colangelo & G. A. Davis (Eds.), *Handbook of gifted education*. Allyn & Bacon.

Gagné, F. (2015). Academic talent development programs: A best practices model. *Asia Pacific Education Review*, 16(2), 281–295.

Gierczyk, M. K. (2017). Pojęcie „zdolność" w narracji studentów angielskich i polskich: ujęcie kognitywne. *Studia Edukacyjne*, 45. https://doi.org/10.14746/se.2017.45.14

Gierczyk, M. K. (2019). *Uczeń zdolny w polskiej i angielskiej przestrzeni szkolnej: Studium komparatystyczne* (No. 3882). Wydawnictwo Uniwersytetu Śląskiego.

Gierczyk, M. K. & Dyrda, B. (2018). Indywidualizacja pracy dydaktyczno-wychowawczej z uczniem zdolnym: doświadczenia brytyjskie. In *Nie)codzienność indywidualizacji w przestrzeni wczesnoszkolnej inny w ławce szkolnej* (Vol. 2, pp. 25–50). Adam Marszałek.

Gierczyk, M. K. & Hornby, G. (2021). Twice-exceptional students: Review of implications for special and inclusive education. *Education Sciences*, 11(2), Article 2. https://doi.org/10.3390/educsci11020085

Gierczyk, M. K. & Pfeiffer, S. I. (2021). Retrospective view of gifted British and Polish college students: The impact of school environment on talent development. *Journal of Advanced Academics*, 32(4). https://doi.org/10.1177/1932202X211034909

Hany, E. A. (1993). How teachers identify gifted students: Feature processing or concept-based classification. *European Journal for High Ability*, 4.

Harris, P., Smith, B. M. & Harris, J. J. (2011). *The myths of standardized tests: Why they don't tell you what you think they do*. Rowman & Littlefield.

Hays, E. A. (2016). *Academic outcomes in higher education for students screened as twice-exceptional: Gifted with a learning disability in math or reading* (Doctoral dissertation). University of Tennessee.

Heylighen, F. (1992). A cognitive-systemic reconstruction of Maslow's theory of self-actualization. *Behavioral Science*, 37.

Hodges, J., Tay, J., Maeda, Y. & Gentry, M. (2018). A meta-analysis of gifted and talented identification practices. *Gifted Child Quarterly*, 62(2), 147–174. https://doi.org/10.1177/0016986217752107

Jacobs, J. & Archie, T. (2008). Investigating sense of community in first-year college students. *Journal of Experiential Education*, 30(3), 282–285. https://doi.org/10.1177/105382590703000312

Jansen, D., Petry, K., Ceulemans, E., Noens, I. & Baeyens, D. (2017). Functioning and participation problems of students with ASD in higher education: Which reasonable accommodations are effective? *Journal of Special Needs Education*, 32(1), 71–88. https://doi.org/10.1080/08856257.2016.1254962

Kaufman, S. B. & Sternberg, R. J. (2008). Conceptions of giftedness. In S. I. Pfeiffer (Ed.), *Handbook of giftedness in children*. Springer.

King, S. (2022). The education context for twice-exceptional students: An overview of issues in special and gifted education. *Neurobiology of Learning and Memory*, 193, 107659.

Konstantopoulos, S., Modi, M. & Hedges, L.V. (2001). Who are America's gifted? *American Journal of Education*, 109(3), 344–382.

Kranz, A. E., Serry, T. A. & Snow, P. C. (2024). Twice-exceptionality unmasked: A systematic narrative review of the literature on identifying dyslexia in the gifted child. *Dyslexia*, 30(1), e1763. https://doi.org/10.1002/dys.1763

Lee, K. M., & Olenchak, F. R. (2015). Individuals with a gifted/attention deficit/hyperactivity disorder diagnosis: Identification, performance, outcomes, and interventions. *Gifted Education International*, 31(3).

Lewandowski, L., Lovett, B. J., Gordon, M. & Antshel, K. (2006). The case for clinical impairment in the DSM–V criteria for ADHD. *The ADHD Report*, 14(6), 8–15.

Limont, W. (2008). Model struktur zdolności kierunkowych i jego implikacje teoretyczne i praktyczne. In W. Limont, J. Cieślakowska & J. Dreszer (Eds.), *Zdolności. Talent. Twórczość. Tom 1*. Wydawnictwo Naukowe UKM.

Limont, W. (2010). *Uczeń zdolny: Jak go rozpoznać i jak z nim pracować*. GWP.

Little, T. (2014). Exams aren't everything, says Eton headmaster. *RadioTimes*, 13 August. http://www.radiotimes.com/news/2014-08-13/exams-arent-everything-says-eton-headmaster [accessed 1 January 2025]

Madaus, J., Cascio, A., Delgado, J., Gelbar, N., Reis, S. & Tarconish, E. (2023). Improving the transition to college for twice-exceptional students with ASD: Perspectives from college service providers. *Career Development and Transition for Exceptional Individuals*, 46(1), 40–51. https://doi.org/10.1177/21651434221091230

Maddocks, D. L. (2018). The identification of students who are gifted and have a learning disability: A comparison of different diagnostic criteria. *Gifted Child Quarterly*, 62(2), 175–192. https://doi.org/10.1177/0016986217752096

Maddocks, D. L. (2020). Cognitive and achievement characteristics of students from a national sample identified as potentially twice exceptional (gifted with a learning disability). *Gifted Child Quarterly*, 64(1), 3–18.

McCallum, R. S., McClurg, V. M. & Wu, J. (2021). Academic success of general education college students compared to those screened as twice-exceptional and gifted. *Innovative Higher Education*, 46(4), 411–427. https://doi.org/10.1007/s10755-021-09543-z

McClurg, V. M., Wu, J. & McCallum, R. S. (2021). Academic success of general education college students compared to those screened as twice-exceptional and gifted. *Innovative Higher Education*, 46(4), 411–427. https://doi.org/10.1007/s10755-021-09543-z

Mönks, F. J. & Heller, K. A. (1994). Identification and programming of the gifted and talented. In T. Husén & T. N. Postlethwaite (Eds.), *The international encyclopedia of education* (Vol. 5, 2nd ed.). Pergamon.

Moon, S. M. (2003). Personal talent. *High Ability Studies*, 14(1), 5–21.

Moon, S. M. (2006). Developing a definition of giftedness. In J. Purcell & R. Eckhart (Eds.), *A guidebook for developing educational services and programs for gifted and talented students*. Corwin Press.

Morelock, M. J. (1996). On the nature of giftedness and talent: Imposing order on chaos. *Roeper Review*, 19(1), 4–12.

Morin, A. (2018). Seven myths about twice-exceptional students. In *Understood for Learning and Attention Issues* [online]. https://www.understood.org/en/friends-feelings/empowering-your-child/building-on-strengths/7-myths-about-twice-exceptional-2e-students [accessed 1 January 2025]

Morrison, W. F. & Rizza, M. G. (2007). Creating a toolkit for identifying twice-exceptional students. *Journal for the Education of the Gifted*, 31(1), 57–76. https://doi.org/10.4219/jeg-2007-513

Muglia Wechsler, S., Palmeira Pereira, V. L. & Delou, C. M. C. (2024). Educating the gifted in Brazil: Analysis from a learning-resource perspective. *Cogent Education*, 11(1). https://doi.org/10.1080/2331186X.2024.2327761

National Research Council. (2002). *Minority students in special and gifted education*. The National Academies Press. https://doi.org/10.17226/10128

Paton, G. (2009). Bright pupils "agonising" over simple questions, says Eton head. *The Telegraph*. http://www.telegraph.co.uk/education/educationnews/4938107/Bright-pupils-agonising-over-simple-questions-says-Eton-head.html [accessed 1 January 2025]

Pfeiffer, S. I. (2015). *Essentials of gifted assessment*. Wiley.

Phelps, R. P. (2009). *Kill the messenger: The war on standardized testing*. Transaction Publishers.

Popek, S. (2001). *Człowiek jako jednostka twórcza*. UMCS.

Raoof, K., Shokri, O., Fathabadi, J. & Panaghi, L. (2024). Unpacking the underachievement of gifted students: A systematic review of internal and external factors. *Heliyon*, 10(17), e36908. https://doi.org/10.1016/j.heliyon.2024.e36908

Reider Lewis, L. (2021). Twice-exceptionality: Maximizing academic and psychosocial success in youth. *Journal of Health Service Psychology*, 47(3), 191–196. https://doi.org/10.1007/s42843-021-00046-1

Reis, S. M., Baum, S. M. & Burke, E. (2014). An operational definition of twice-exceptional learners: Implications and applications. *Gifted Child Quarterly*, 58(3), 217–230. https://doi.org/10.1177/0016986214534976

Reis, S. M., Gelbar, N. W. & Madaus, J. W. (2022). Understanding the academic success of academically talented college students with autism spectrum disorders. *Journal of Autism and Developmental Disorders*, 52(10), 4426–4439. https://doi.org/10.1007/s10803-021-05290-4

Reis, S. M. & McCoach, D. B. (2002). Underachievement in gifted and talented students with special needs. *Exceptionality*, 10(2), 113–125. https://doi.org/10.1207/S15327035EX1002_5

Reis, S. M., McGuire, J. M. & Neu, T. W. (2000). Compensation strategies used by high-ability students with learning disabilities who succeed in college. *Gifted Child Quarterly*, 44(2), 123–134. https://doi.org/10.1177/001698620004400205

Reis, S. M., Neu, T. W. & McGuire, J. M. (1997). Case studies of high-ability students with learning disabilities who have achieved. *Exceptional Children*, 63(4), 463–479. https://doi.org/10.1177/001440299706300403

Renzulli, J. S. (1978). What makes giftedness? Re-examining a definition. *Phi Delta Kapan*, 60(3), 180–184. https://doi.org/10.1177/003172171109200821

Renzulli, J. S. (1984). The triad/revolving door system: A research-based approach to identification and programming for the gifted and talented. *Gifted Child Quarterly*, 28(4), 163–171. https://doi.org/10.1177/001698628402800405

Renzulli, J. S. (2005). The Three-Ring Conception of Giftedness: A developmental model for promoting creative productivity. In R. J. Sternberg & J. E. Davidson (Eds.), *Conceptions of giftedness* (2nd ed., pp. 246–279). Cambridge University Press. https://doi.org/10.1017/CBO9780511610455.015

Renzulli, J. S., & Reis, S. M. (1997). *The schoolwide enrichment model: A comprehensive plan for educational excellence*. Creative Learning Press.

Rinn, A. N. (2007). Effects of programmatic selectivity on the academic achievement, academic self-concepts, and aspirations of gifted college students. *Gifted Child Quarterly*, 51(3), 232–245. https://doi.org/10.1177/0016986207302718

Rizza, M. G. & Morrison, W. F. (2007). Identifying twice-exceptional children: A toolkit for success. *TEACHING Exceptional Children Plus*, 3(3).

Rocha, A., Borges, Á., García-Perales, R. & Almeida, A. I. S. (2024). Differences in socio-emotional competencies between high-ability students and typically developing students. *Frontiers in Education*, 9, 1450982. https://doi.org/10.3389/feduc.2024.1450982

Ronksley-Pavia, M. (2015). A model of twice-exceptionality: Explaining and defining the apparent paradoxical combination of disability and giftedness in childhood. *Journal for the Education of the Gifted*, 38(1).

Sandoval-Rodríguez, K. & Conejeros-Solar, M. L. (2024). Voices of twice-exceptional students in their first year of higher education. *Gifted and Talented International*, 39(1), 60–69. https://doi.org/10.1080/15332276.2024.2340025

Silverman, L. K. (2000). The two-edged sword of compensation: How the gifted cope with learning disabilities. In K. Kay (Ed.), *Uniquely gifted: Identifying and meeting the needs of the twice-exceptional student* (pp. 153–159). Avocus.

Snyder, K. H., McClurg, V. M., Wu, J. & McCallum, R. S. (2020). Success of students screened as twice-exceptional as a function of major selection and academic strength. *Journal of Advanced Academics*, 46(4).

Sternberg R. J. (2003): WICS as a model of giftedness. *High Ability Studies*, 14(2).

Sternberg, R. J., Jarvin, L. & Grigorenko, E. L. (2010). Giftedness and culture. In *Explorations in Giftedness* (pp. 144–167). Cambridge University Press.

Subotnik, R. F., Olszewski-Kubilius, P. & Worrell, F. C. (2011). Rethinking giftedness and gifted education: A proposed direction forward based on psychological science. *Psychological Science in the Public Interest*, 12(1), 3–54.

Tourreix, E., Besançon, M. & Gonthier, C. (2023). Non-cognitive specificities of intellectually gifted children and adolescents: A systematic review of the literature. *Journal of Intelligence*, 11(7), 141. https://doi.org/10.3390/jintelligence11070141

Trail, B. A. (2022). *Twice-exceptional gifted children: Understanding, teaching, and counseling gifted students*. Routledge.

Vaivre-Douret, L. (2011). Developmental and cognitive characteristics of "high-level potentialities" (highly gifted) children. *International Journal of Pediatrics*, 2011, 420297. https://doi.org/10.1155/2011/420297

Webb, J. T., Amend, E. R., Webb, N. E., Goerss, J., Beljan, P. & Olenchak, F. R. (2019). Misdiagnosis and dual diagnosis of gifted children. SENG, 10 January. https://www.sengifted.org/post/misdiagnosis-and-dual-diagnosis-of-gifted-children

Webb, J. T., Amend, E. R., Webb, N. E., Goerss, J., Beljan, P. & Olenchak, F. R. (2005). *Misdiagnosis and dual diagnosis of gifted children and adults*. Great Potential Press.

White, S. W., Elias, R., Salinas, C. E., Capriola, N., Conner, C. M., Asselin, S. B., Miyazaki, Y., Maefsky, C. A., Howlin, P. & Getzel, E. E. (2016). Students with autism spectrum disorder in college: Results from a preliminary mixed methods needs analysis. *Research in Developmental Disabilities*, 56, 29–40. https://doi.org/10.1016/j.ridd.2016.05.010

Yssel, N., Speirs Neumeister, K. & Burney, V. (2020). Students with special needs who are gifted and talented (twice exceptional). In *Oxford research encyclopedia of education*. https://oxfordre.com/education/view/10.1093/acrefore/9780190264093.001.0001/acrefore-9780190264093-e-1218

# Students With Selected Disabilities – Implications for Work

# Two

## INTRODUCTION

Higher education is a key stage in the life of many, and a time characterized by increased demands, opportunities for personal development and identity formation. It is a time for self-exploration, confronting adulthood and gaining skills for independence, often for the first time. It is also a transition from the role of a student (who is still legally under the care of parents/guardians) to that of an "academic student" (independent, defining their existence). This is often a pivotal moment that not only involves changes associated with leaving behind one's previous lifestyle, habits and rules; it is also a time to focus on the necessity of coping with various situations, often stepping out from under the protective parental umbrella, overcoming barriers and confronting personal limitations (Bełza et al., 2018).

### Dual Roles and Identity Formation

For individuals with disabilities, this transition presents unique challenges that go beyond those experienced by their peers. These individuals often assume dual roles, both as students and as persons with disabilities, positioning them at the intersection of social expectations and personal aspirations. This duality influences how they experience education at the higher education level, shaping not only their academic paths but also a broader sense of self and integration within academic communities. It also translates into building self-confidence and shaping self-image. This situation also leads to the formation of a dual identity. As indicated in Ronksley-Pavia's double exceptionalism model (see Chapter 1), disability is a characteristic that places individuals in the category of double exceptionality; however, it often comes to the forefront, leading to a person with a disability being vulnerable to marginalization, stereotypical treatment and even exclusion (Lee & Olenchak, 2015).

DOI: 10.4324/9781003571674-2

## The Impact of Expectations and Unconscious Bias

Relating this to Rosenthal and Jacobson's (1968a) concept of social expectations, how we think about individuals with disabilities and how we approach them can condition and influence their educational success. In the 1960s, Robert Rosenthal and Lenore Jacobson (1968a) demonstrated in their experiment how teacher expectations can influence student achievements. The Pygmalion effect (Rosenthal & Jacobson, 1968b) works on the principle that it acts as a kind of "trigger" for certain reactions or outcomes. If educators and families think about a given student in a stereotypical way, it influences their behaviours towards that student. We send signals to them, which are sometimes unconscious on our part, but which can elicit certain feedback reactions. If this is negative thinking, as in the Golem Effect (Babad et al., 1982), and we do not expect high results from the student, behaviours change. For example, we might lower our standards, assess students more leniently, and fail to tolerate behaviours that may be unacceptable in other students. We also fail to motivate and raise self-esteem, excuse and ultimately accept a lower level, even if the student is capable of more. This discrepancy can create a self-fulfilling prophecy, in which students adapt to these expectations and consequently achieve lower academic results (McKown & Weinstein, 2008; Shepherd, 2011). In contrast, when we have higher expectations for students we consider more capable, we smile more often, have more empathy and encourage them to be proactive. If they fail at something, we explain it as a temporary weakness, encourage them more and are more willing to raise their grades, as in the Galatea Effect (see Babad et al, 1982).

It is crucial to address the unconscious biases that may influence teacher expectations. Yssel et al. (2016) emphasize the importance of professional development initiatives focused on raising awareness and equipping teachers with tools to set positive, inclusive expectations. This training can serve as a remedy for biases, providing teachers with the foundations for more empathetic and constructive engagement with students with disabilities. For these students to reach their potential, it is important to recognize and nurture their intellectual strengths while appropriately considering their disabilities (Willard-Holt, 1999).

The socio-cultural transformations and associated emancipation of people with disabilities in recent decades have led to a greater participation of disabled students in higher education, enabling their voices and perspectives to become a more visible part of academic discourse. However, their inclusion is typically accompanied by persistent barriers and challenges. For example, students with disabilities often encounter lowered expectations that reflect doubts about their ability to meet academic standards. In contrast, there is a tendency to push back, expecting successful outcomes from these students, as if they need to prove their place in the academic environment. Both extremes can significantly undermine the positive educational outcomes of disabled students, limiting their opportunities and reinforcing institutional inequalities. These complexities highlight the importance of exploring how both positive and negative expectations affect the effectiveness, identity and outcomes of disabled students.

This chapter analyses research literature from both theoretical and empirical perspectives in the fields of inclusive education, disability studies and educational psychology. The theoretical concept guiding these reflections is the interpersonal expectation effect identified by Rosenthal, providing insight into how academic attitudes and peer dynamics can shape the academic outcomes of students with disabilities. Furthermore, the analysis of double exceptionalities emphasizes the need for tailored pedagogical strategies to support students whose potential is often overshadowed by their disabilities. The results of these analyses aim to identify practical strategies for fostering inclusive learning environments and strengthening institutional practices that promote equity.

**UNDERSTANDING STUDENTS WITH DISABILITIES IN HIGHER EDUCATION: DUAL ROLES AND CHALLENGES RELATED TO IDENTITY**

Research on the experiences of twice-exceptional students in higher education is complex, with intersections of identity, expectations and institutional dynamics. Students with disabilities face unique challenges in higher education, navigating dual roles that require them to integrate their identities as students with the social and academic perceptions of their disabilities. This duality often results in challenges related to self-identification and social integration. As Dolmage (2017) posits, these dual roles stem from social and institutional pressures that expect conformity to traditional student norms while simultaneously highlighting the distinctiveness of students' disabilities. This tension often leads students to struggle with a conflict between their academic and social identities. They may wish to function solely in the role of a student, yet their environment often "pushes" them into the role of a disabled student (cf. Gajdzica, 2011). The social pressure to balance both roles – one as a capable student and the other as someone dealing with a disability – requires significant emotional and psychological effort. These competing expectations can limit their ability to fully engage in academic life and lead to feelings of otherness, making it difficult for them to integrate into the academic environment as equal participants (Dolmage, 2017).

### Stigma and Disclosure Dilemmas

As a result, students may feel compelled to conform to unrealistic academic standards, which increases the risk of burnout and decreases their sense of self-efficacy. These institutional shortcomings highlight the need for a paradigm shift in higher education's approach to integrating and including students with disabilities. Shifting the focus from conformity to adaptability can foster a sense of belonging among students, and allow them to navigate their dual identities without compromising their self-worth.

Social stigma surrounding disability adds another layer of complexity, as students often internalize negative societal perceptions, prompting them to either mask their disabilities or overperform academically. This phenomenon is well documented by Marshak et al. (2010), who point out that students may forgo necessary accommodations to avoid being perceived as less capable by their peers or faculty. This not only impacts their academic success but also deepens feelings of inadequacy and isolation. The stigmatizing effect of disability further reinforces a culture where students with disabilities feel compelled to meet heightened expectations, often at the expense of their well-being.

Given these challenges, institutions must actively work to dismantle stigma through awareness programmes, mentorship opportunities and peer networks. These initiatives can foster inclusivity and promote an environment where students feel valued for their contributions, independent of their disabilities. Additionally, the reluctance of students with disabilities to disclose their condition presents significant barriers to utilizing necessary educational resources.

Disclosure is often avoided due to the fear of negative reactions or discriminatory treatment from faculty and peers, as described by Marshak et al. (2010). This reluctance is compounded by insufficient awareness of available support systems, which leaves many students uncertain about the benefits of disclosure. Research suggests that inclusive academic cultures – where disability is normalized – encourage higher rates of disclosure, enabling students to access essential accommodations (Marshak et al., 2010).

### Patterns of Self-Identification

So, many students continue to choose different options regarding their self-identification as a person with a disability. Often, these identities are associated with one of the following types of students with disabilities:

- the exhibitionist student (openly discussing their disability, considering it an asset that gives them a pass to various accommodations);
- the "visible incognito" student (entering the academic community as an able-bodied student, not openly talking about their disability, yet their behaviours reveal certain characteristics identifying them with a disability);
- the "invisible incognito" student (their disability features are so invisible and do not hinder activities that they can remain anonymous about their disability);
- the "normal" student (entering the community with the behaviours of an able-bodied person but not hiding the fact that they are a person with a disability, considering that disability can be regarded as just one of the characteristics that defines them) (Bełza et al., 2017).

However, research by Woods and Lindeman (2008) suggests that students who disclose their disability often experience greater support and inclusion, while concealing a disability may be associated with a higher level of stress and social isolation. Therefore, colleges should create spaces that eliminate prejudice and support integrative practices for students, so that they can disclose their needs without fear of stigmatization. These strategies are essential to ensure equal access to education and improve the academic experiences of students with disabilities.

### The Twice-Exceptional Challenge

Gifted students with disabilities encounter additional challenges due to their dual exceptionalities, which complicate efforts to balance their academic potential with the need for accommodations. Willard-Holt (1999) underscores the discrepancy between the intellectual capabilities of these students and the emphasis placed on their disabilities, which often masks their potential. Traditional methods of evaluating giftedness fail to accommodate dual exceptionalities, as disabilities can hinder students' test performance and classroom participation. Identifying and supporting these students requires an overhaul of conventional criteria to uncover and cultivate their talents. Furthermore, Willard-Holt (1999) argues that misaligned expectations from faculty and peers exacerbate this issue, as educators may focus excessively on the disability while neglecting the intellectual growth of these students.

Each disability, apart from certain difficulties or limitations on one side, has certain talents and increased abilities on the other side. It is important to raise awareness in academic communities about abilities and talents, as this will help prevent the entrenchment of stereotypes towards people with disabilities, which often have a pejorative connotation. These, as Neuberg (2013) argues, can serve as interpersonal expectations in themselves, loosely defined as beliefs that a person will possess a certain trait or ability or act in a certain way. It is worth examining the social perception of people with specific disabilities in relation to their abilities and talents to make it clear that, in addition to the stereotypically viewed difficulties faced by people with a certain disability, they may gain increased capabilities in another area through a compensatory mechanism. The stereotypical difficulties of individuals with a given disability are outlined below, as compared with the potential that makes them twice-exceptional.

Disability is undoubtedly associated with certain individual needs. But, in addition to these needs, increased abilities in some area can be identified in many people. Although this is not the case for all people with a particular disability, it is the responsibility of teachers, as well as support services, to identify the potential that a student has. Being aware of the balancing act between the difficulties arising from the disability and what the student may be good at will increase the student's chances of merging their dual identity and reaching their maximum potential, both intellectually and socio-emotionally.

For students with autism spectrum disorders (ASDs), the challenges extend beyond academics to include difficulties with social interactions and integration into peer networks. Van Hees et al. (2015) note that students with ASD often have difficulty interpreting social cues, making social interactions in academic settings exhausting and intimidating. The rigidity of traditional academic environments, which typically lack the flexibility to adapt to the unique needs of these students, further limits their ability to engage effectively. These limitations contribute to isolation, loneliness and reduced opportunities to make meaningful connections. Inclusive academic practices, such as peer mentoring programmes and structured group activities, can serve as essential tools for bridging this gap and fostering a supportive community for students with ASD (Van Hees et al., 2015). Personalized support mechanisms, including dedicated counsellors or autism specialists, can also help these students navigate social norms and academic systems, increasing their participation and confidence.

Students with hearing disabilities as a result of compensating for their inability to perceive auditory stimuli also have unique talents and abilities that can be their strengths in academic education. Research has shown that the brains of deaf people can process visual data better, which promotes greater attention to detail in the environment. Due to auditory perception of information, they are more proficient in non-verbal communication and lip reading, as this is a key tool for interaction (Marschark et al., 2013). Due to difficulties in different areas and having to deal with a reality that is not always adapted to their needs, they can be more flexible and creative in finding solutions and dealing with problems. Creativity, for which many of them operate on a high level, can be seen in multiple fields of art, such as painting, theatre and sculpture (Potmesilova et al., 2024). It is worth taking into account their uniqueness and talents, in many cases representing an invaluable contribution to various areas of life, during the teaching process.

Students with dyslexia also have their potential in addition to specific learning difficulties. It is said that dyslexia is a gift (Davis & Braun, 2010), which is related to the specific abilities and capacities it provides. The strengths of people with dyslexia can include verbal skills, particularly in storytelling and verbal reasoning, which is due to compensatory strategies for coping with learning difficulties (Shaywitz, 2003). They find it easier to solve problems and are more creative, which has a respected place in many areas (Reid, 2016). Research by Eide and Eide (2011) shows that many of these individuals excel in visual-spatial tasks, think outside the box and innovate. Hence, "Understanding the strengths of dyslexic students is crucial to their academic success and personal development" (Reid, 2016).

### Creating Inclusive Academic Environments

The dual roles and identity challenges faced by students with disabilities in higher education are shaped by a complex interaction of personal, social and systemic factors. Meeting these challenges requires a multifaceted approach that includes fostering inclusive academic cultures, eliminating stigma and providing tailored support mechanisms. By recognizing and valuing their dual uniqueness, universities can create environments in which these students can develop as equal participants.

## THE ROSENTHAL EFFECT AND ACADEMIC EXPECTATIONS

The Rosenthal effect, as already noted in the introduction, shows how social and teacher expectations can profoundly shape the academic performance and self-perception of students, including those with disabilities. This psychological phenomenon highlights how positive expectations from teachers can improve students' academic performance by influencing their teaching behaviour. These expectations are always associated with specific behaviours that are based on the knowledge, experiences and stereotypes that teachers hold. Brophy and Good (1970) illustrated the process of interpersonal expectations, as presented in Figure 2.1.

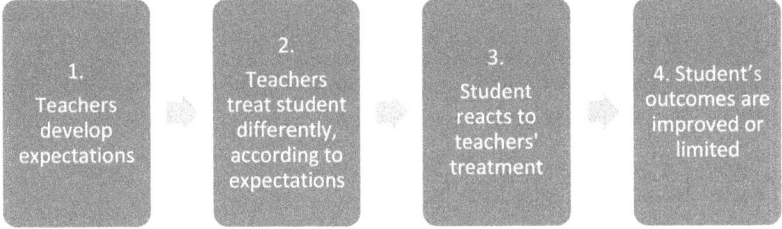

**Figure 2.1** Process model of teacher expectations on student outcomes as proposed by Brophy and Good (1970)

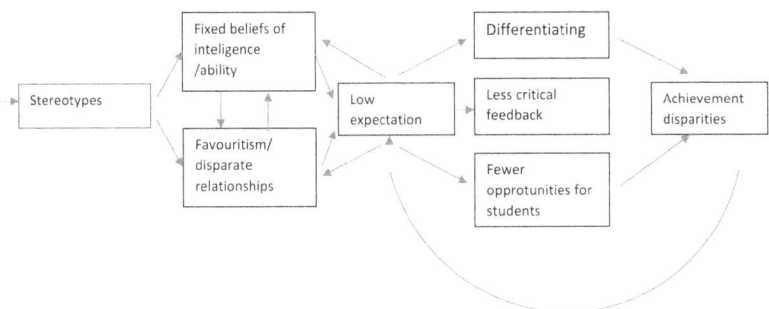

**Figure 2.2** Updated process model

The model in Figure 2.1 shows a simplified diagram of teacher expectations as proposed in the 1970s. Subsequent years have seen the evolution of this model, which has been expanded to include processes relevant to these relationships. Among other things, the type of expectations and associated behaviour of teachers has been taken into account.

Impacts on Students With Disabilities

In the case of students with disabilities, this dynamic is particularly relevant, as teacher attitudes and expectations often determine whether students feel empowered or marginalized in the academic environment. High expectations can result in increased encouragement, access to resources, and intellectual challenge, thus fostering both improved academic performance and increased self-esteem (Rosenthal, 2002). However, the opposite is also true: when teachers have lower expectations, students are often overlooked, receive less attention and are exposed to less intellectual stimulation. This perpetuates poor performance, limits opportunities for skill development and lowers self-efficacy (Dolmage, 2017). The Rosenthal effect is therefore a double-edged sword, and its positive or negative impact largely depends on teachers' attitudes.

In the case of students with disabilities, this dynamic is particularly relevant, as teacher attitudes and expectations often determine whether students feel empowered or marginalized in the academic environment. High expectations can result in increased encouragement, access to resources and intellectual challenge, thus fostering both improved academic performance and increased self-esteem (Rosenthal, 2002). However, the opposite is also true: when teachers have lower expectations, students are often overlooked, receive less attention and are exposed to less intellectual stimulation. This perpetuates poor performance, limits opportunities for skill development and lowers self-efficacy (Dolmage, 2017). The Rosenthal effect is therefore a double-edged sword, and its positive or negative impact largely depends on teachers' attitudes.

### The Self-Fulfilling Prophecy

A central element to the Rosenthal effect is the concept of a self-fulfilling prophecy, in which students internalize and act on expectations set by teachers or social norms. When these expectations are constructive, students with disabilities are more likely to demonstrate increased self-efficacy, enabling them to overcome barriers to success. Positive reinforcement not only results in better academic performance but also contributes to greater satisfaction with the educational experience (Dolmage, 2017; Rosenthal, 2002). Conversely, negative expectations lead to reduced motivation and poor academic performance as students internalize the belief that they are inherently less capable. Setting high but fair expectations ensures that the demands are sufficient while students are not overwhelmed, enabling them to align their achievement with their potential (Willard-Holt, 1999). Institutional policies, such as the implementation of the Universal Design for Learning (UDL) framework, can further assist teachers in creating inclusive classroom environments that support the success of students with disabilities (Dolmage, 2017).

### Negative Manifestations and Consequences

The negative manifestations of the Rosenthal effect are equally important, especially when academic staff inadvertently lower expectations or reduce instructional rigor for students with disabilities. This can convey implicit messages of incompetence, reducing students' self-esteem and reinforcing external stereotypes about their abilities (Dolmage, 2017; Yssel et al., 2016). Furthermore, the lack of equitable challenges limits students' ability to grow intellectually, further limiting their academic trajectories. Willard-Holt (1999) argues that unconscious biases related to perceptions of disability often lead teachers to prioritize ease over equity, thus neglecting opportunities for skill development. These challenges highlight the importance of ongoing critical reflection among teachers, along with systemic interventions such as disability awareness workshops to mitigate the negative effects of the Rosenthal effect and promote equality in academic practices (Dolmage, 2017).

Gifted students with disabilities, often described as having dual exceptionalities, experience unique challenges that exemplify the profound impact of the Rosenthal effect. Their intellectual abilities are often obscured by the focus on their disability, resulting in a gap between potential and academic performance. Willard-Holt (1999) describes how an overemphasis on disability hinders the identification of giftedness, thereby inhibiting their cognitive development. The Rosenthal effect similarly emphasizes the importance of balanced expectations that recognize both strengths and challenges, enabling these students to excel without being defined solely by their disability (Rosenthal, 2002). Failure to identify and nurture the intellectual abilities of students with dual exceptionalities often excludes them from gifted programmes and limits their opportunities for academic growth (Willard-Holt, 1999). To remedy this, institutions need to adopt tailored support strategies that combine advanced instruction with necessary accommodations, fostering a holistic approach to education that values their unique potential (Dolmage, 2017).

### Fostering Self-Determination

Encouraging self-determination among students with disabilities is another key strategy for mitigating the negative effects of the Rosenthal effect. Research shows that students who develop self-determination skills and proactively engage with teachers about their needs achieve better academic performance and greater satisfaction (Yssel et al., 2016). Self-determination enables students to effectively articulate their requirements, allowing them to be more proactive in their academic journey. Training that focuses on supporting self-determination can further create a supportive environment where students feel confident disclosing their needs without fear of stigmatization (Dolmage, 2017). Proactive disclosure promotes transparency and collaboration between students and teachers, ensuring that adjustments are mutually agreed-upon and effective (Yssel et al., 2016). In addition, university-wide initiatives such as workshops, mentoring programmes and streamlined facility request processes can provide students with the resources they need to deal effectively with academic challenges (Dolmage, 2017).

## STUDENTS' EXPECTATIONS OF THE ACADEMIC ENVIRONMENT

Students with disabilities have specific expectations of their academic environments in order to ensure equal access and successful participation in higher education. One of the most important expectations is the provision of appropriate and individualized facilities tailored to their specific needs to facilitate equal opportunities in their educational pursuits. When these facilities are missing, or poorly implemented, students experience significant barriers to academic progress that hinder their engagement and achievement. Marshak et al. (2010) highlight how those inadequate facilities, such as delayed access to materials or inadequate technological support, can fundamentally undermine student experience and performance outcomes.

We live in an era of new technologies that contribute significantly to making higher education more accessible. Adaptive technologies, such as screen readers for visually impaired students and speech-to-text conversion software for those with motor impairments (Yssel et al., 2016), assistive listening devices (induction loops, FM systems, etc.), transcription and audio description of teaching materials, allow students to bridge the gap between their individual needs and academic requirements. However, structural shortcomings, such as limited institutional commitment or insufficient faculty awareness, further exacerbate the challenges faced by students with disabilities

(Marshak et al., 2010). Such shortcomings highlight the critical need for a personalized approach to designing adaptations to meet the diverse needs in this group.

As argued by Yssel et al. (2016), it is essential to tailor support to individual circumstances – while a student with a learning disability may benefit from visual aids, another may require detailed written instructions. Addressing these gaps requires a coordinated institutional effort to support inclusion and ensure that all students can thrive.

### Faculty Attitudes and Teaching Practices

The other main expectation of students with disabilities relates to the attitudes and practices of lecturers. The understanding and proactive approach of lecturers in meeting diverse needs plays a critical role in shaping the success of these students. Positive interactions with lecturers who use inclusive teaching methods, such as using visual and audio materials to enhance accessibility, are highly valued and are associated with better educational outcomes (Yssel et al., 2016).

On the other hand, Marshak et al. (2010) identify faculty resistance as a significant barrier to student success, often stemming from prejudice or inadequate disability training. This resistance contributes to an environment in which students may feel undervalued or marginalized. To mitigate these barriers, academic staff need to take a proactive approach, not only in providing facilities but also in promoting a culture of equality and values.

Dolmage (2017) highlights the importance of incorporating diversity-sensitive practices into teaching methods to challenge stereotypes and foster a sense of collective belonging.

### Inclusive Campus Culture

Expectations of inclusivity extend beyond interactions in the classroom to include institutional policies and campus culture. Students expect universities to actively promote awareness and inclusivity, thereby fostering environments that reduce stigma and foster a sense of belonging. Oertle et al. (2017) found that a positive campus climate significantly increases student satisfaction and retention rates by cultivating a supportive community. Such environments encourage students to seek resources and engage more effectively, which has a particular impact on students with disabilities who might otherwise feel excluded.

An integral part of the academic experience is the expectation of independence and self-determination. Students with disabilities place a high value on environments that empower them, rather than adopting overly protective practices that are seen as detrimental to their development. While lecturers and peers may act with good intentions, overprotective behaviors can reinforce negative social narratives of dependency and undermine students' confidence in their abilities (Yssel et al., 2016). By fostering independence, academic environments can play a key role in supporting students' sense of self-efficacy and resilience, thereby improving both academic and social outcomes.

Mentoring programs and structured support initiatives that focus on building problem-solving and resilience skills can help strike a balance between providing necessary accommodations and encouraging independent decision-making. Oertle et al. (2017) emphasize that environments that promote empowerment and self-determination significantly contribute to students achieving their potential. However, misconceptions and stereotypes can hinder this dynamic, leading to alienation and exclusion (Dolmage, 2017).

To counter these barriers, universities must foster mutual understanding by organizing diversity workshops or academic clubs for individuals interested in developing within specific fields. Another key expectation is for institutions to provide comprehensive information and resources regarding available services and accommodations. Marshak et al. (2010) found that students often remain unaware of the full scope and quality of disability services due to ineffective communication from the university. This lack of awareness results in underutilization of essential resources and directly impacts academic performance. Broader dissemination of information, for example, through poster campaigns, digital platforms and student support services, can bridge this gap and ensure equal access to assistance (Marshak et al., 2010).

### Meeting the Needs of Twice-Exceptional Students

The expectations of twice-exceptional students – those who combine intellectual giftedness with a disability – add another layer of complexity to the discourse. Willard-Holt (1999) identifies widespread frustration among these students, as their intellectual potential is often overshadowed by their disability. This oversight results in limited academic opportunities and disengagement, indicating that their needs are not being adequately met. A balanced approach that recognizes and nurtures both their intellectual strengths and need for accommodations is fundamental to their academic success (Willard-Holt, 1999). Tailored educational policies and teaching strategies can help bridge the gap between potential and outcomes. Van Dinther et al. (2011) stress the need for teacher training to identify and nurture the abilities of twice-exceptional students, ensuring they receive both the recognition and support necessary for growth. Integrating disability and giftedness into a cohesive support system has the potential to revolutionize the academic experience of these students, effectively addressing their unique needs and expectations.

The expectations of students with disabilities toward their academic environment span multiple dimensions, from individualized accommodations and faculty attitudes to campus climate and peer interactions. To effectively meet these expectations, universities must adopt comprehensive and inclusive strategies that address the structural, social and individual barriers faced by students.

## THE INFLUENCE OF FACULTY MINDSETS ON EDUCATIONAL ACCESSIBILITY

### Training Gaps and Misconceptions

Academic staff expectations and attitudes towards students with disabilities often reflect the influence of the medical model of disability, which emphasizes individual impairments over the need for systemic restructuring. This perspective reinforces the narrative that disabilities are personal challenges rather than institutional or societal failures that require systemic solutions. As a result, academic staff may focus predominantly on addressing impairments rather than reconsidering and improving curricula or teaching methods to foster inclusivity. Bunbury (2018) argues that such an approach perpetuates attitudes that stigmatize students with disabilities, hinder innovation in pedagogy and position inclusive practices as secondary priorities. Moreover, this emphasis on impairments disregards how systemic changes – such as UDL approaches – could benefit all learners, not only students with disabilities (Bunbury, 2018; Dolmage, 2017).

Claiborne et al. (2011) suggest that integrating a needs-based framework from the social model of disability could help academic staff address systemic inequities and remove barriers. Training focused on the social model has been shown to shift staff perspectives, facilitating the adoption of inclusive practices such as UDL (Yssel et al., 2016). However, the persistence of the medical model within higher education underscores the need for continued efforts to reshape institutional attitudes and redefine inclusion as a systemic responsibility rather than an individualized challenge.

Bunbury (2018) and Dolmage (2017) emphasize that comprehensive, evidence-based training is essential to eliminate misconceptions among faculty members. Such training should focus on the rationale and fairness of accommodations and their role in promoting equitable participation and academic success. Without addressing these biases, faculty attitudes may reinforce stereotypes about the abilities of students with disabilities, influencing their self-perception and academic engagement (Dolmage, 2017; Stanczak et al., 2023).

### The Challenge of Non-Disclosure

A major challenge in promoting inclusivity is the widespread underestimation of the presence of students with disabilities, primarily due to the non-disclosure of certain conditions. Matthews (2009) highlights how non-disclosure – often driven by fear of stigma or negative treatment – leads instructors to adopt a uniform classroom dynamic that overlooks the diversity of student needs. This issue is especially pronounced for students with "invisible" disabilities, such as dyslexia or chronic illnesses, who may not require formal accommodations (Fuller et al., 2004; Matthews, 2009). The result is a lack of inclusive teaching practices that could account for the heterogeneity of students' experiences (Bunbury, 2018).

Matthews (2009) and Claiborne et al. (2011) advocate for systemic solutions, such as encouraging disclosure through confidential communication channels or anonymous reporting tools. Targeted administrative interventions – such as mandatory training programmes that incorporate experiential learning about disability – are also important (Bunbury, 2018). Additionally, providing appropriate resources and clear institutional guidelines can reduce faculty resistance and build awareness of the uniqueness of individuals with specific disabilities (Claiborne et al., 2011).

### Unconscious Bias and Academic Expectations

Unconscious biases among lecturers may lead to lowered academic expectations for students with disabilities, negatively affecting their self-esteem and academic outcomes. Stanczak et al. (2023) point out that such biases often reinforce stereotypes that associate disability with limited academic ability, thereby influencing the level of academic rigor and challenge presented to these students. This form of bias aligns with the Rosenthal effect, which illustrates how low expectations can lead to self-fulfilling prophecies, where students internalize reduced standards and perform worse academically (Dolmage, 2017; Rosenthal, 2002). Conversely, setting high – but realistic – expectations has a positive impact on academic achievement and self-efficacy, as demonstrated by Yssel et al. (2016). Therefore, it is essential that university faculty challenge students with disabilities while simultaneously providing the necessary support for them to succeed.

## BEYOND ACCOMMODATION: STRATEGIC SUPPORT FOR STUDENTS WITH DUAL EXCEPTIONALITIES

Educating twice-exceptional students – those who have both a disability and giftedness – requires a nuanced understanding of their unique needs and potential in order to develop appropriate support strategies. Several key elements make up the foundation of supporting twice-exceptional students in academic environments.

### Balancing Support With Intellectual Challenge

Recognizing and nurturing the potential of students with disabilities is essential in supporting twice-exceptional individuals in higher education. These students often need to balance managing their disability with academic demands and personal aspirations – a balance between one identity and another. Willard-Holt (1999) argues that disproportionate focus on accommodations – although necessary – may inadvertently overshadow the cognitive strengths of these students.

**Tailored educational approaches**, such as differentiated instruction, help strike this balance by adapting to various learning styles and perceptions, enabling twice-exceptional students to achieve academic excellence. Differentiated instruction also allows educators to design activities that address individual strengths and challenges, fostering an environment where academic potential is not compromised by disability-related accommodations. Dolmage (2017) emphasizes that such an approach is essential for uncovering hidden talents and ensuring that students are not defined solely by their disabilities. By integrating innovative teaching methods, universities can offer more holistic support that aligns with the dual needs of these students. Creating an environment that simultaneously acknowledges intellectual abilities and addresses disability is critical to ensuring that students are not limited by preconceived notions of their capabilities and expectations. Research suggests that environments focusing on strengths rather than limitations lead to better academic and socio-emotional outcomes, as positive reinforcement fosters confidence and drives achievement (Mihut et al., 2020).

**Teacher attitudes** play a crucial role in realizing this shift, as educators who focus on students' potential rather than their disabilities help break down stereotypes and promote inclusion. Dolmage (2017) emphasizes that academic communities trained to identify and nurture student potential play a vital role in creating equitable educational opportunities.

### Reimaging Assessment for Hidden Talents

Identifying giftedness among students with disabilities remains a significant challenge due to limitations in traditional assessment tools and methods. Standardized tests – often designed to measure abilities in ways that disadvantage students with disabilities – fail to account for the impact of disability on test results.

**Meaningfully modifying these tools is important** to uncover the hidden potential of twice-exceptional students (Willard-Holt, 1999). For instance, alternative assessment methods such as dynamic testing or portfolio-based evaluations may reveal hidden talents more effectively than conventional methods. These approaches allow for a broader and more nuanced understanding of giftedness by considering the unique compensatory skills developed by students with disabilities.

Montgomery (2009) highlights that compensatory skills – such as problem-solving or creativity, often developed as coping mechanisms –

should be central to giftedness criteria. Unfortunately, traditional measures often overlook these indicators, leaving many gifted students unrecognized.

### Training Educators to Recognize Dual Exceptionality

**Teacher and evaluator training** is crucial for supporting inclusive identification practices. Educators must be better prepared to recognize non-traditional signs of giftedness and interpret them in the context of a student's disability. Gierczyk and Hornby (2021) stress the importance of professional development programmes that equip educators to identify and support twice-exceptional students.

**Observational methods** – such as monitoring group interactions and evaluating contributions to group projects – can offer insight into students' intellectual potential that might otherwise remain hidden (Montgomery, 2009). Moreover, redefining giftedness to include diverse expressions of intelligence is essential for addressing the underrepresentation of twice-exceptional students.

Studies indicate that teachers often prioritize addressing disability over nurturing intellectual strengths, which limits students' opportunities to fully develop their talents (Gierczyk & Hornby, 2021). To counteract this, training should emphasize strategies that balance accommodations with intellectual development support.

For example, designing curricula that challenge students while also addressing disability-related needs can promote both dimensions of twice-exceptionality. Collaborative training initiatives involving general educators, special educators and gifted education specialists offer another path toward a more integrated support approach in higher education. These initiatives can provide alternative strategies for engaging students and creating inclusive environments.

**Including case studies** in training programmes can further highlight effective practices and their tangible outcomes, motivating teachers to adopt similar strategies (Willard-Holt, 1999). Students with disabilities – especially those who are twice-exceptional – often use their intelligence to bypass challenges, masking both the extent of their disability and the range of their abilities. This paradox creates a gap between students' true potential and their academic outcomes, necessitating proactive interventions to effectively address it (Willard-Holt, 1999). For example, training faculty to recognize subtle signs of intelligence may help uncover hidden talents and tailor teaching strategies accordingly (Montgomery, 2009).

The paradox of hidden abilities also affects how students perceive themselves, reinforcing the importance of mentoring programmes and reflective practices that help students understand and embrace their twice-exceptionality. Such interventions can enhance both self-esteem and academic success, fostering an environment where students feel valued and supported (Mihut et al., 2020).

**Peer support programmes** can encourage understanding between twice-exceptional students and their non-disabled peers (Dolmage, 2017).

### Creating Inclusive Learning Environments

**Assistive technologies** offer valuable tools for uncovering intellectual strengths while mitigating the effects of disability. These technologies, designed specifically for twice-exceptional students, help create equitable academic environments by focusing on empowerment and adaptability (Montgomery, 2009). Collectively, these strategies aim to create a balanced approach that addresses the complexity of twice-exceptionality. Using assistive technologies, such as real-time adaptation software and adaptive keyboards, is another crucial element in ensuring that all students – regardless of ability – can actively participate in both physical and virtual learning environments (Burgstahler, 2021; Dolmage, 2017).

**Expectations of parents and teachers** play a key role in shaping the academic outcomes of twice-exceptional students. Research by Mihut et al. (2020) shows that high but realistic expectations enhance social-emotional and academic success, while overly high or low expectations can negatively impact performance and self-esteem.

**Mentoring programmes involving successful twice-exceptional graduates can serve as aspirational models** while also offering guidance to parents and educators (Willard-Holt, 1999). Mentoring programmes that pair students with disabilities with staff or senior students offer valuable guidance, helping them effectively navigate academic challenges and set realistic goals (Willard-Holt, 1999).

**Inclusive learning environments** further support the identification of students' potential. Designing education based on the principles of Universal Design for Learning enables equal access by addressing diverse needs. For example, alternative assessments, proactive faculty engagement, and diverse instructional materials ensure that twice-exceptional students can thrive (Dolmage, 2017). Moreover, integrating UDL strategies – such as offering multiple means of engagement and representation – supports varied learning preferences. For example, combining visual aids with traditional lectures increases accessibility and enriches the educational experience for all students (Burgstahler, 2021). Likewise, designing assignments that allow for varied formats – such as essays, multimedia projects or presentations – enables fair assessment of student skills.

### Balancing Support With Independence

**Balancing high yet realistic expectations** for students with disabilities cannot be overstated. The Rosenthal effect highlights the significance of teachers' expectations in shaping student outcomes, as high expectations can foster self-efficacy and academic achievement (Thurlow & Quenemoen, 2019). It is essential to emphasize the need for training that increases awareness and competence regarding the impact of expectations, ensuring that teachers' attitudes positively influence students' confidence and performance (Dolmage, 2017). Showcasing the achievements of twice-exceptional students – through awards or recognition ceremonies, for instance – further enhances self-efficacy and motivates continued effort (Thurlow & Quenemoen, 2019).

All of the above-described elements represent essential implications for creating safe, accepting learning environments in higher education – crucial for meeting the diverse needs of students, especially those who are twice-exceptional with disabilities. This requires a multidimensional approach, including the principles of UDL, proactive faculty training and the cultivation of supportive environments that encourage disclosure and peer collaboration. **Encouraging the disclosure of disability** within a supportive environment is another cornerstone of non-discriminatory education. Non-disclosure is often driven by fear of stigma or negative treatment, which can lead to unmet educational needs (Matthews, 2009).

To address this issue, universities must normalize discussions around disability and create safe spaces that promote openness. Misconceptions and stereotypes about disability – such as presumed lower competence – must also be challenged to foster a truly inclusive institutional culture. Peer education programmes that highlight diversity and inclusion can help break down these biases and strengthen empathy among students (Griffin et al., 2012).

Collaborative educational initiatives promote academic engagement and reduce bias by emphasizing the meaningful contributions of all participants. Ongoing evaluation of inclusive policies and student feedback mechanisms ensures the refinement and effectiveness of these strategies (Burgstahler, 2021). By addressing both systemic and individual challenges faced by twice-exceptional students, institutions can create environments where potential is not only recognized but fully realized.

## CONCLUSION

The accessibility of higher education for people with disabilities requires universities to recognize and respond to the unique challenges faced by twice-exceptional (2e) students with disabilities – individuals who experience significant learning differences but also possess remarkable talents (Soares Coutinho-Souto & de Souza Fleith, 2022; Ness & Price, 1990). These students, who may struggle with learning difficulties (such as those stemming from dyslexia or autism), often face challenges in adapting to conventional learning environments, and they may have difficulty following instructions, course content or materials (Yenduri et al., 2023). However, it is crucial to acknowledge that every disability also brings certain strengths that can be harnessed to support academic success and personal development (Soares Coutinho-Souto & de Souza Fleith, 2022).

Educational inclusion is a complex and multidimensional process that depends on the active involvement of the entire educational community (Coutinho-Souto & de Souza Fleith, 2022). To effectively support these students, universities should adopt a multifaceted approach that includes inclusive teaching strategies, assistive technologies and a supportive academic environment (Rudisel, 2009). Institutions must also work on raising awareness among academics and other community members about the unique characteristics of students with disabilities. It is essential to understand that a student with a disability is first and foremost a student; their disability may require support in certain areas, but in others, we may benefit from their talents and strengths. This path to success involves abandoning the stereotypical lens of the medical model of disability in favour of recognizing the individual's potential, and reflecting on what we, as educators, can contribute to this interaction in order to achieve pedagogical success – through the success of our student.

This is possible by creating inclusive academic environments that address the diverse learning styles and needs of twice-exceptional students. These environments are capable not only of identifying students' needs for support but also of recognizing and nurturing their unique gifts and talents. Achieving this requires moving away from traditional teaching methods and embracing creative instructional strategies that engage students facing challenges related to learning, attention and self-regulation (Rudisel, 2009).

Study time for many people with disabilities is not only a time of change but a redefinition of their self-perception. It would seem that this is a period during which one can shed the stigma of being a person with a disability and begin to be seen through the prism of one's abilities, rather than limitations or the "prime" feature that labels someone as disabled (Bełza-Gajdzica, 2019). Therefore, it is important to pursue various means to normalize the perception of students with disabilities within academic spaces – not through the lens of disability as stigma, but rather through the perspective of disability as uniqueness.

## REFERENCES

Babad, E. Y., Inbar, J., & Rosenthal, R. (1982). Pygmalion, Galatea, and the Golem: Investigations of biased and unbiased teachers. *Journal of Educational Psychology*, 74(4), 459–474. https://doi.org/10.1037/0022-0663.74.4.459

Bełza, M., Gajdzica, Z. & Prysak, D. (2017). (Nie)łatwe drogi wchodzenia w dorosłość przez osoby z niepełnosprawnością. Wydawnictwo Arka.

Bełza, M., Gajdzica, Z. & Prysak, D. (2018). (Nie)łatwe drogi wchodzenia w dorosłość. Wydawnictwo Arka.

Bełza-Gajdzica, M. (2019). Infrahumanisation of students with disabilities (a case study). *Kultura-Społeczeństwo-Edukacja*, 2, 71–83. DOI:10.14746/kse.2019.16.5

Brophy, J. & Good, T. (1970). Teacher communication of differential expectations for children's classroom performance: Some behavioral data. *Journal of Educational Psychology*, 61, 365–374. https://doi.org/10.1037/h0029908

Bunbury, S. (2018). Niepełnosprawność w szkolnictwie wyższym: czy racjonalne dostosowania przyczyniają się do włączającego programu nauczania? *International Journal of Inclusive Education*, 1–30. https://dx.doi.org/10.1080/13603116.2018.1503347

Burgstahler, S. (2021). *Ramy dla praktyk włączających w szkolnictwie wyższym*. University of Washington. https://www.washington.edu/doit/sites/default/files/atoms/files/A%20Framework%20for%20Inclusive%20Practices%20in%20Higher%20Education_.pdf

Claiborne, L. B., Cornforth, S., Gibson, A. & Smith, A. (2011). Wspieranie studentów z upośledzeniami w szkolnictwie wyższym: Integracja społeczna czy zimny komfort? *International Journal of Inclusive Education*, 15(5), 513–527. https://doi.org/10.1080/13603110903131747

Czerwińska, K. (2019). Proces stawania się innym – bohater filmu fabularnego tracący wzrok. *Kultura i Edukacja*, 123(1), 296–311. DOI:1015804/kie.2019.01.18

Davis, R. D. & Braun, E. M. (2010). *The gift of dyslexia, revised and expanded: Why some of the smartest people can't read . . . and how they can learn*. Penguin.

Dolmage, J. T. (2017). *Akademicki ableizm: Niepełnosprawność i szkolnictwo wyższe*. University of Michigan Press. http://dx.doi.org/10.3998/mpub.9708722

Domagała-Zyśk, E. (2021). Model projektowania uniwersalnego w akademickiej edukacji inkluzyjnej. Strategie i rekomendacje. In *Oblicza życia. Księga Jubileuszowa Profesor Doroty Kornas-Bieli*. Wydawnictwo Episteme.

Dycht, M. (2016). Myths and stereotypes related to people with visual disability. In *Forum pedagogiczne* (pp. 297–316). Uniwersytet Kardynała Stefana Wyszyńskiego w Warszawie.

Eide, B. L. & Eide, F. (2011). *The dyslexic advantage: Unlocking the hidden potential of the dyslexic brain*. Hudson Street Press.

Fuller, M., Healey, M., Bradley, A. & Hall, T. (2004). Barriers to learning: A systematic study of the experience of disabled students in one university. *Studies in Higher Education*, 29(3), 303–318. https://doi.org/10.1080/0307507041006815925 92

Gajdzica, Z. (2011). *Sytuacje trudne w opinii nauczycieli klas integracyjnych*. Impuls – UŚ Kraków – Katowice.

Gibson, S. (2012). Narrative accounts of university education: Socio-cultural perspectives of students with disabilities. *Disability & Society*, 27(3), 353–369. https://doi.org/10.1080/09687599.2012.654987

Gierczyk, M. & Hornby, G. (2021). Twice-exceptional students: Review of implications for special and inclusive education. *Education Sciences*, 11(2), 1–10. https://doi.org/10.3390/educsci11020085

Grandin, T. (2023). *Visual thinking: The hidden gifts of people who think in pictures, patterns, and abstractions*. Penguin.

Grandin, T. & Panek, R. (2013). *The autistic brain: Thinking across the spectrum*. Houghton Mifflin Harcourt.

Griffin, M. M., Summer, A. H., McMillan, E. D., Day, T. L. & Hodapp, R. M. (2012). Attitudes toward including students with intellectual disabilities at college. *Journal of Policy and Practice in Intellectual Disabilities*, 9(4), 234–239. https://doi.org/10.1111/jppi.12008

Jankowiak, B., Bujalska, D., Kondzior, D., Kowalewska, B., Rolka, H., Klimaszewska, K. & Krajewska-Kułak, E. (2015). Postawy społeczeństwa wobec osób chorych psychicznie. In W. E. Krajewska-Kułak, C. Łukaszuk, J. Lewko & W. Kułak (Eds.),

*W drodze do brzegu życia*. T. 13. *Praca zbiorowa* (pp. 599–613). Uniwersytet Medyczny w Białymstoku. Wydział Nauk o Zdrowiu.

Knopik, T., Papuda-Dolińska, B., Wiejak, K. & Krasowicz-Kupis, G. (2021). Projektowanie uniwersalne jako perspektywa metodyczna edukacji włączającej. *Niepełnosprawność*, 42, 53–69.

Lee, K. M., & Olenchak, F. R. (2015). Individuals with a gifted/attention deficit/hyperactivity disorder diagnosis: Identification, performance, outcomes, and interventions. *Gifted Education International*, 31(3), 185–199.

Marschark, M., Morrison, C., Lukomski, J., Borgna, G. & Convertino, C. (2013). Are deaf students visual learners? *Learning and Individual Differences*, 25, 156–162.

Marshak, L., Van Wieren, T., Ferrell, D. R., Swiss, L. & Dugan, C. (2010). Exploring barriers to college student use of disability services and accommodations. *Journal of Postsecondary Education and Disability*, 22(3), 151–163. https://files.eric.ed.gov/fulltext/EJ906688.pdf 31

Matthews, N. (2009). Teaching the "invisible" disabled students in the classroom: Disclosure, inclusion, and the social model of disability. *Teaching in Higher Education*, 14(3), 229–239. https://www.ru.ac.za/media/rhodesuniversity/content/equityampinstitutionalculture/images/Teaching_the_invisible_disabled_students_in_the_classroom_disclosure_inclusion_and_the_social_model_of_disability.pdf

McKown, C. & Weinstein, R. S. (2008). Modeling the Role of child ethnicity and gender in children's differential response to teacher expectations. *Journal of Applied Social Psychology*, 32(1), 159–184. https://doi.org/10.1111/j.1559-1816.2002.tb01425.x

Mihut, G., McCoy, S. & Maître, B. (2020). Academic and socio-emotional outcomes of young people with special educational needs and the role of parental educational expectations (Working Paper No. 692). Economic and Social Research Institute, Trinity College Dublin. https://www.esri.ie/system/files/publications/WP692.pdf

Montgomery, D. (2009). Special educational needs and dual exceptionality. In *The Routledge international companion to gifted education* (p. 8). Routledge. https://www.taylorfrancis.com/chapters/edit/10.4324/9780203609385-32/special-educational-needs-dual-exceptionality-diane-montgomer y

Ness, J. & Price, L. A. (1990). Meeting the psychosocial needs of adolescents and adults with LD. *Intervention in School and Clinic*, 26(1), 16–20.

Neuberg, S. L. (2013). Proces potwierdzania oczekiwań w interakcjach obciążonych stereotypami. In S. Trusz (Ed.), *Efekt oczekiwań interpersonalnych. Wybór tekstów*. Wydawnictwo Naukowe Scholar.

Norman, L. J. & Thaler, L. (2018). Human echolocation for target detection is more accurate with emissions containing higher spectral frequencies, and this is explained by echo intensity. *i-Perception*, 9(3), 1–18.

Oertle, K. M., Fleming, A. R., Plotner, A. J. & Hakun, J. G. (2017). Influence of social factors on student satisfaction among college students with disabilities. *Journal of College Student Development*, 58(2), 215–228. https://vtechworks.lib.vt.edu/bitstreams/8ac4b923-80c0-48f9-acf6-6e45678d2161/download

Płatos, M., Cychowska, M., Płucienniczak, K. & Pisula, E. (2023). *Uczelnia dostępna dla studentów ze spektrum autyzmu. Podręcznik dla specjalistów, nauczycieli akademickich i osób zarządzających w edukacji wyższej.* Centrum Wsparcia Dydaktyki Uniwersytetu Warszawskiego.

Plutecka, K. (2009). Social reception of chronically hard of hearing people – Intellectual myths and stereotypes. In T. Żółkowska & I. Ramik-Mażewska (Eds.), *Special pedagogy in researches and scientific analysis*. University of Stettin Special Pedagogy Department.

Podgórska-Jachnik, D. (2019). Psychospołeczne konteksty ADHD. In K. Sipowicz, A. Witusik & T. Pietras (Eds.), *ADHD Wybrane zagadnienia diagnozy i terapii* (pp. 167–180). Wrocław.

Potmesilova, P., Potmesil, M. & Klugar, M. (2024). Differences between the creativity of people who are deaf of hard of hearing and those with typical hearing: A protocol for the further scopin review. *Creativity Studies, 17*(1).

Raport, C. B. O. S. (2021). Społeczny obraz autyzmu. Raport z badań ilościowych zrealizowanych przez Fundację CBOS dla Fundacji JiM.

Reid, G. (2016). *Dyslexia: A practitioner's handbook.* Wiley.

Rosenthal, R. (2002). Chapter 2 – The Pygmalion effect and its mediating mechanisms. *Educational Psychology*, 25–36. https://doi.org/10.1016/B978-012064455-1/50005-1

Rosenthal, R. & Jacobson, L. (1968a). *Teacher expectation and pupils' intellectual development.* Holt, Rinehart & Winston.

Rosenthal, R. & Jacobson, L. (1968b). Pygmalion in the classroom. *Urban Rev, 3*, 16–20. https://doi.org/10.1007/BF02322211

Rudisel, C. M. (2009). Working with atypical learners. *Changing English, 16*(4), 413–416. https://doi.org/10.1080/13586840903392003

Shaywitz, S. (2003). *Overcoming dyslexia: A new and complete science-based program for reading problems at any level.* Alfred A. Knopf.

Shepherd, M. A. (2011). Effects of ethnicity and gender on teachers' evaluation of students' spoken responses. *Urban Education, 46*(5), 1011–1028. https://doi.org/10.1177/0042085911400325

Soares Coutinho-Souto, W. K. & de Souza Fleith, D. (2022). Sobredotación y TDAH: una revisión sistemática de la literatura. *Revista De Psicología, 40*(2), 1175–1211. https://doi.org/10.18800/psico.202202.019

Stanczak, A., Aelenei, C., Pironom, J., Toczek, M.-C., Rohmer, O. & Jury, M. (2023). Can students with special educational needs overcome the "success" expectations? *Social Psychology of Education*, 1–23. https://doi.org/10.1007/s11218-023-09806-x

Thurlow, M. L. & Quenemoen, R. F. (2019). Revisiting expectations for students with disabilities (NCEO Brief #17). National Center on Educational Outcomes. https://nceo.umn.edu/docs/onlinepubs/nceobrief17.pdf

TNTP. (2024). *The impacts of teacher expectations on student outcomes: A practitioner's literature review.* https://tntp.org/wp-content/uploads/2024/09/The-Impacts-of-Teacher-Expectations-on-Student-Outcomes-Literature-Review-2024.pdf

Van Dinther, M., Dochy, F. & Segers, M. (2011). Factors affecting students' self-efficacy in higher education. *Educational Research Review, 6*(2), 95–108. https://doi.org/10.1016/j.edurev.2010.10.003 32

Van Hees, V., Moyson, T. & Roeyers, H. (2015). Higher education experiences of students with autism spectrum disorder: Challenges, benefits, and support needs. *Journal of Autism and Developmental Disorders*, 45(6), 1673–1688. https://biblio.ugent.be/publication/7027122/file/7027143

Willard-Holt, C. (1999). Dual exceptionalities. ERIC EC Digest, #E574, 1–6. ERIC Clearinghouse on Disabilities and Gifted Education. https://citeseerx.ist.psu.edu/document?repid=rep1&type=pdf&doi=7722a7a2655d0481ca034c0c6560ef51cc0f42e4.

Wiśniewska, M. (2017). Słuch osób niewidomych – przegląd badań. *Konteksty kształcenia muzycznego*, 4(2(7)), 97–114. DOI:10.5604/01/3001.0012.1573

Woods, J. & Lindeman, M. (2008). Disability disclosure: The impact of perceptions from peers and professors. *The Journal of Higher Education*, 79(2), 203–221. https://doi.org/10.1353/jhe.0.000

Yenduri, G., Kaluri, R., Rajput, D. S., Lakshmanna, K., Gadekallu, T. R., Mahmud, M. & Brown, D. J. (2023). From assistive technologies to metaverse: Technologies in inclusive higher education for students with specific learning difficulties. *IEEE Access*, May. DOI:10.48550/arXiv.2305.11057

Yssel, N., Pak, N. & Beilke, J. (2016). A door must be opened: Perceptions of students with disabilities in higher education. *International Journal of Disability, Development and Education*, 63(3), 384–394. http://dx.doi.org/10.1080/1034912X.2015.1123232

# Three

Well-Being of Twice-Exceptional and Academically Gifted Students

## INTRODUCTION

As mentioned in Chapter 1, individuals who are gifted in combination with at least one deficit or disability are referred to as twice-exceptional. While it may be difficult to determine the exact size of the twice-exceptional population, it is estimated that about 6% of students who are diagnosed with special education needs may also be gifted (Wood & Estrada-Hernández, 2009).

Most research regarding twice-exceptionality focuses on school-aged children and adolescents, due to the fact that identifying and supporting such students appears to be crucial in the early stages of education. There is little research on university students due to the lack of systematic identification of such individuals. A limited awareness of the specifics of twice-exceptionality is another issue with less research attention. Twice-exceptional students often arrive at universities with high scores (e.g. in matriculation exams/as winners of Olympiads), thus giving the impression of being well adjusted and successful. However, many face challenges, particularly in the area of mental health, that have been misunderstood, ignored or underestimated during their years in school (Hill, 2020). They may also be students who were characterized as mediocre in the enrollment process as a result of neglect, or excessive focus on deficits, at previous stages of education of the development of their abilities (Smyth, 2017). Therefore, understanding the well-being of twice-exceptional persons requires insight into their experiences and the challenges they face.

## STUDENT WELL-BEING

To date, the concept of well-being does not have an agreed-upon precise definition, so different concepts of well-being are based on different indicators. The notion of well-being grew out of two

DOI: 10.4324/9781003571674-3

different philosophical perspectives. The first, a hedonistic one, focuses on subjective, cognitive and positive evaluations of life. Well-being in this concept results from the presence of satisfaction and positive feelings, such as happiness, and the absence of negative feelings, such as worries (Hossain et al., 2023). The second perspective, eudaimonic, refers to the functioning and development of a person's potential. It is associated with engaging in activities that are valuable and aligned with an individual's goals (Thorsteinsen & Vittersø, 2018). According to Donald and Jackson (2022), well-being for university students includes both hedonistic (achieving pleasure and avoiding pain) and eudaimonic (a sense of meaning and authenticity) aspects. For the purposes of the chapter, I will use the World Health Organization's (WHO) definition of well-being, pursuant to which it is defined as "a state . . . in which the individual realizes his or her own abilities, can cope with the normal stresses of life, can work productively and fruitfully, and is able to make a contribution to his or her community" (WHO, 2001).

The well-being of university students is an important issue since it significantly affects their academic success and overall life satisfaction (Cotton et al., 2002). Academic performance is strongly linked to students' psychological well-being. Educational success (good grades, credits) contributes to feelings of satisfaction and overall well-being, while academic difficulties can lead to stress, anxiety and lowered mood. Research indicates that students with good and very good academic performance express higher levels of satisfaction and well-being, and are more likely to use stress-coping strategies that are focused on problem-solving. In contrast, students with mediocre or unsatisfactory results are more likely to feel dissatisfied with various aspects of their personality, have difficulty adjusting to the demands of their environment and use avoidance strategies (Trucchia et al., 2013). The interplay between well-being and academic success is complex, with research indicating an important role for psychological, motivational and environmental factors, such as agreeableness, conscientiousness and openness to experience (Osamika et al., 2021), positive attitudes, self-acceptance, control over the environment, autonomy, ability to maintain positive relationships with others (Mustafa et al., 2020) or university commitment (Yu et al., 2018).

Academic adjustment as well as intrinsic motivation and satisfaction with the study programme are of particular importance and serve as key predictors of persistence and success (Rooij et al., 2018). In addition, well-being is influenced by factors related to the university, such as relationships with other students, lecturers, the availability of psychological support and the organization of education (Eloff et al., 2022). A stressful academic environment adversely affects mental health, while early detection and intervention for mental health problems positively influences student success (Garces et al., 2024). Positive self-esteem in a university environment and academic passion, such as being enthusiastic about one's education, are significant motivators, prompting students to become more engaged in their studies and improving their overall study experience (Johari & Ahmad, 2019). Moreover, external factors like family relationships, social support and financial situation also impact well-being (Eloff et al., 2022). Support from peers and family reduces anxiety and contributes to feelings of belonging and happiness (Jiménez et al., 2018; Putri & Novitasari, 2017), so students with strong social ties cope better with stressors (Rodríguez et al., 2020).

In conclusion, students' well-being is determined by a complex web of inter-relationships among their mental health, social support and level of engagement in learning. Therefore, universities should take a holistic approach that considers all of these aspects to effectively support their students. This can be achieved through well-targeted support programmes as well as thoughtful academic policies and measures to create a campus culture that is healthy and promotes learning.

## CHALLENGES OF BEING A TWICE-EXCEPTIONAL PERSON AND THEIR IMPACT ON WELL-BEING

The well-being of twice-exceptional students who are both gifted and have special educational needs requires a nuanced understanding of their unique challenges and strengths as well as addressing childhood experiences, which are strongly linked to a sense of well-being in adulthood (Bellis et al., 2013).

### Lack of/Incorrect Diagnosis

Firstly, some adults were never diagnosed as twice-exceptional (2e). For some, talents may have hidden the challenges of deficits, resulting in their difficulties not being recognized in childhood. Other students may have struggled academically, performed poorly or experienced social-emotional problems despite their high potential (Minnaert, 2022). Students who were not identified as 2e in childhood may not be recognized as twice-exceptional at the tertiary level either, as the individual's disability may mask their talent, or vice versa (Baldwin et al., 2015). According to Peters (2015), even a late diagnosis allows one to better understand one's limitations and realize one's potential more fully. It's worth mentioning that the concept of twice-exceptionality is relatively unknown, which can result in the fact that both society and adults themselves may not be aware that their struggles stem from a combination of high abilities and specific challenges. Secondly, even if individuals were diagnosed in childhood, this does not imply that they received adequate care and suport – many educational systems have a gap in resources and guidance systems that are unable to address the complex needs of 2e children. This can have lasting effects on the well-being of twice-exceptional adults (Besnoy et al., 2015), as they may carry unresolved childhood issues into their adult lives.

### Impact of Early School Experiences and Labelling

Early school experiences are vital to an individual's subsequent educational paths and achievements. Negative experiences can result in giving up, while positive ones help develop ways to cope with challenges. Educational systems that focus on students of average ability essentially discriminate against 2e students (Lo & Yuen, 2015). The early educational experiences of those with twice-exceptionalities can often be difficult and frustrating. Teachers unprepared to work with such students label them as lazy, unmotivated or naughty (Wood & Estrada-Hernández, 2009). Freebern (2023) notes that what may look like laziness or insufficient effort to teachers is actually a double effort for the 2e student to use their potentials to hide deficits in order to perform like their average peers. Twice-exceptional individuals who were not recognized in childhood, or who did not receive adequate support, may find it difficult to access higher education, since the gap between actual performance and expected progress increases with age, as the material becomes more demanding (Spicer, 2011).

### Self-Perception of 2e Individuals

Research emphasizes the importance of positive self-esteem among children, and its impact on long-term success. The self-esteem of students with twice-exceptionality is largely shaped by the labelling and educational experiences outlined above. According to a study by Barber and Mueller (2011), 2e adolescents were characterized by less positive self-concepts compared to their gifted or unidentified peers. Lummiss' (2018) research showed that twice-exceptional students perceive their talents and difficulties as separate elements. A sense of belonging to a group of gifted students appeared when they discussed their strengths, while identification with a group of students with difficulties emerged when they reflected weaknesses. They often felt different from others, which affected their self-esteem in various areas. Some respondents regretted that they had not been diagnosed or that they received the diagnosis too late, while others perceived their educational experience as positive. The author highlighted that the use of gifted/disabled labels can result in social and emotional difficulties. Labels affect how society views individuals; however, they also impact how those individuals view themselves.

### Social and Emotional Challenges

Individuals with twice-exceptionality are often highly critical of themselves and have low self-esteem, especially with regard to their academic performance. They may have difficulty balancing conflicting messages about their abilities and disabilities (Wood & Estrada-Hernández, 2009). They experience feelings of loneliness and challenges in building social relationships, which, for those undiagnosed in childhood, prompts them to seek a diagnosis in adulthood (Peters, 2015). The sense of otherness, the challenges faced and the inability to integrate socially can lead to feelings of isolation or failure in social situations (Sengil-Akar & Akar, 2020). Research conducted by Lummiss (2018) found that 2e students experience barriers in forming friendships, are objects of teasing, prefer solitude and feel exhausted in social interactions. In addition, according to the study, twice-exceptional students' social experiences are associated with being victims of bullying and social isolation, which has a profound impact on their mental health. Experiencing bullying, especially in school settings, intensifies feelings of inadequacy and leads to emotional distress (Ronksley-Pavia et al., 2018). The sense of being trapped by one's deficits, inability to realize one's potential and lack of acceptance from the environment can lead to self-destructive behavior (Spicer, 2011).

### Family Support

Family support constitutes a key factor influencing the development of twice-exceptional students. It is important to emphasize the complexity of the experience of parents of 2e persons – on the one hand, their child's disability affects their emotions as well as relationships with other family members and the economic situation, and on the other hand, they face challenges related to the talent/ability label. Lo and Yuen (2015) highlight that the family plays an essential role in neutralizing negative educational experiences, helping to cope with frustrations and difficulties encountered at school/university. In addition, family support is crucial for motivation and self-esteem, boosts confidence in strengths and helps in setting goals. High parental expectations (which should not be equated with excessive pressure) can also motivate students to develop their talents.

### Educational Barriers and Lack of Adequate Support

It is possible that twice-exceptional students experience a lack of support tailored to their specific needs at the university level. Higher education institutions may not offer differentiated instruction and assistance that focuses on strengths and compensates for disabilities (Cain et al., 2019; Ronksley-Pavia, 2015), which can reflect on academic success, which is linked to a sense of well-being. In addition, research indicates that twice-exceptional individuals may have high cognitive abilities, yet their self-esteem or skills may not match actual academic demands, which may affect their mental health (Foley-Nicpon et al., 2015). Twice-exceptional students may particularly struggle to fit into traditional educational systems, as it is not uncommon for them to lack social skills or face misunderstandings due to their disabilities. However, research suggests that addressing the social-emotional needs of twice-exceptional students is critical to their overall academic achievement (Spicer, 2011).

In conclusion, twice-exceptional university students may struggle with the same problems as school children, such as inadequate interventions or lack of support, as well as new challenges arising from entering adulthood. Their well-being is related to receiving education and support that compensates for deficits and allows them to develop their strengths. Recognition of capabilities and talents can positively influence the growth of self-confidence, awareness of one's own potential and motivation to achieve goals. On the other hand, labels associated with giftedness can have a negative impact – increasing perfectionism, pressure and creating a sense of difference or isolation (Perrone et al., 2007). Students whose potential masks deficits may experience disappointment: related to studying, fatigue from the effort put into hiding weaknesses, gender role conflicts and interpersonal difficulties (Willings, 1985). However, many of those whose deficits mask ability may not perform at a level commensurate with their talents. As Freebern (2023) notes, "while an average person may eventually reach their full potential, a twice exceptional person can often envision exceptional potential without the ability to reach it. Life becomes a series of 'could-have-beens'." It is possible that 2e adults should consider their careers as two separate spheres: a professional area and an area of creative growth (Willings, 1985), according to their abilities and needs.

**RESEARCH PROJECT**

The aim of the research for this chapter was to fill the gap in the source literature on the well-being of twice-exceptional students. The first goal of the project was to diagnose twice-exceptionalism (the size and nature of the phenomenon) within a group of Polish students. As a criterion for being a twice-exceptional student, the respondent's declaration of having special educational needs and academic achievements was adopted, such as well-being, receiving an academic scholarship, authorship or co-authorship of academic publications, participation in research projects or received awards related to academic activities.

Many gifted adults were never identified as gifted in childhood (e.g. identification by teacher or specialist diagnosis) and were unaware of their own potential (Silverman, 2009); therefore the second goal of the project was to assess the perceptions of their own talents and giftedness by both twice-exceptional students and students without this characteristic.

Since the research conducted so far demonstrates the complexity of twice-exceptionality, linking it to potential emotional and social problems, and, consequently, lower well-being (Minnaert, 2022), the third goal of the project was to compare the level of well-being between 2e students and the other student groups.

### Characteristics of the Research Sample

Data was collected through a nationwide survey panel. The research sample consisted of 322 participants with student status. All participants were adults, and their age ranged from 18 to 44 years (M = 23.07). The majority of the sample was female (65.8%, n = 212), with men accounting for 33.5% (n = 108). There were also 0.6% of individuals (n = 2) who declared a different gender identity.

## RESULTS

Statistical analyses were conducted using IBM SPSS Statistics Version 30. Firstly, basic descriptive statistics of the indicators of the variables tested were calculated along with the Shapiro-Wilk normality test. In the next step, analyses of differences were performed using the chi-squared test and one-way analysis of variance. The significance level was taken as the threshold $\alpha = 0.05$; the strength of the effects was interpreted following Cohen's (2016) criteria.

### Academic Achievement and Special Educational Needs

Special educational needs refer to a situation in which an individual requires a special approach in education due to a disability or learning difficulty, such as autism, dyslexia, writing difficulties or above-average ability (Bartnikowska & Antoszewska, 2017). Among all participants, 21.4% reported belonging to the group of people with special educational needs.

Respondents most often reported:

- specific learning difficulties (6.2%);
- behavioral and emotional disorders (5.0%);
- visual disabilities (4.3%);
- hearing disabilities (4.3%).

In addition, 2.5% of participants reported having special talents (of which three respondents also had other special educational needs).

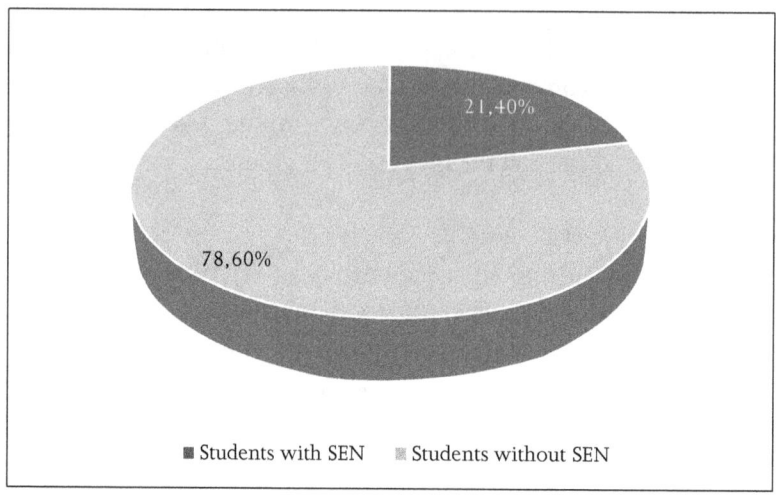

**Figure 3.1** Distribution of respondents by declaration of having special educational needs

Academic achievement refers to the level of success or proficiency achieved in a specific area related to academic work. It is the acquired knowledge or skills developed in particular areas, usually determined by test scores, grades or other indicators. They are used in education to classify and select individuals, provide guidance or measure the effectiveness of learning (Bhat & Bhardwaj, 2014). It should be emphasized that, although academic achievement (AA) is measured by objective indicators, it does not necessarily reflect the full range of a student's abilities. An analysis of respondents' declarations of academic achievement shows that 48.4% reported demonstrating at least one academic achievement.

Among the most frequently declared achievements were receiving a research grant (34.5%) and participating in research projects (19.6%), while 9.9% of respondents were authors or co-authors of scientific publications and 5.9% had been given awards for scientific activities.

Summarizing the data on special educational needs and academic achievements of respondents, it can be concluded that the largest percentage of the study group were students with no SEN (special educational needs) and no academic achievements (44.4%); a slightly smaller number included students declaring academic

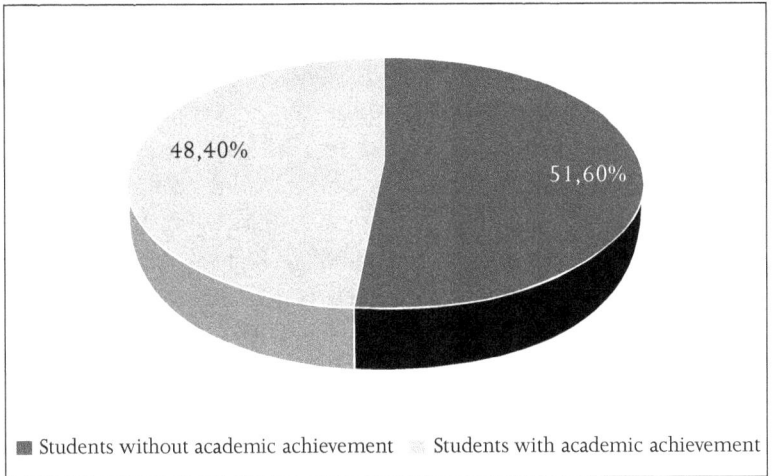

**Figure 3.2** Distribution of respondents by declaration of academic achievement

**Table 3.1** Distribution of respondents by declared special educational needs and academic achievement

| | |
|---|---|
| Twice-exceptional students | 14.3% |
| Students with academic achievement and without SEN | 34.2% |
| Students with SEN and without academic achievement | 7.1% |
| Students without SEN and without academic achievement | 44.4% |

achievements and no special educational needs (34.2%). On average, around one in seven students were twice-exceptional (14.3%), and the smallest group were represented by students declaring having SEN and no academic achievement (7.1%). For the purposes of further analysis, I will apply the abbreviated names for the distinguished groups: students without SEN and without academic achievements, students with academic achievements, 2e students and students with SEN.

In the context of university functioning, the majority of respondents rated their experience positively: 20.5% rated it as very good, 55.3% as rather good and 23.6% as neither good nor bad. Only a few respondents indicated that they rated their functioning as bad or very bad.

Nominations

Nominations represent a method of identifying gifted students, often used in education. We can distinguish between informal nominations, which involve the identification of students by teachers, or formal nominations associated with the use of a list of indicators or scales to identify giftedness. Nominations can be based on the identification of a child not only by a teacher, but also by a parent, an expert, based on academic performance or intelligence tests. A child/person can also make an auto-nomination (Foryś, 2018). In the research presented in this paper, respondents were asked: "Has anyone in the past referred to you as a gifted person?" In the surveyed group, 73.6% of respondents declared that they had heard from their parents that they were gifted, and 73.0% from their teachers (results do not add up to 100% due to the possibility of selecting multiple answers). Opinions about being gifted were also given to respondents by peers (46.0%). Nominations from specialists were reported by respondents less frequently, 13.7% indicated a nomination by a psychologist and 12.1% by a school counsellor. Only 10.9% never encountered such an opinion about themselves. It should be noted that teacher nominations can be subject to the error of preferring students who learn well and do not cause educational problems (Foryś, 2018). Parents, on the other hand, often evaluate their children in a broader context and more emotionally, not necessarily on the basis of skills that are measured in the educational system. Differences in how parents, teachers and the environment perceive a child's abilities may stem from different ways of assessment and the limitations of an educational system that defines talents/abilities restrictively.

Another issue analysed was whether there were differences in nominations by specific individuals in different groups of students. Each variable was compared separately using a chi-squared test of independence, and the results are illustrated collectively in Figure 3.1.

Analysing the results presented in Figure 3.3, it can be concluded that students with academic achievement and students with SEN most often declared that both parents and teachers considered them gifted. However, statistical analysis found no significant differences between the groups (parents $\chi^2(3) = 4.14$, p = 0.247, teachers $\chi^2(3) = 1.64$, p = 0.651), suggesting that opinions were relatively consistent regardless of group specificity. Nominations from peers were also more frequently

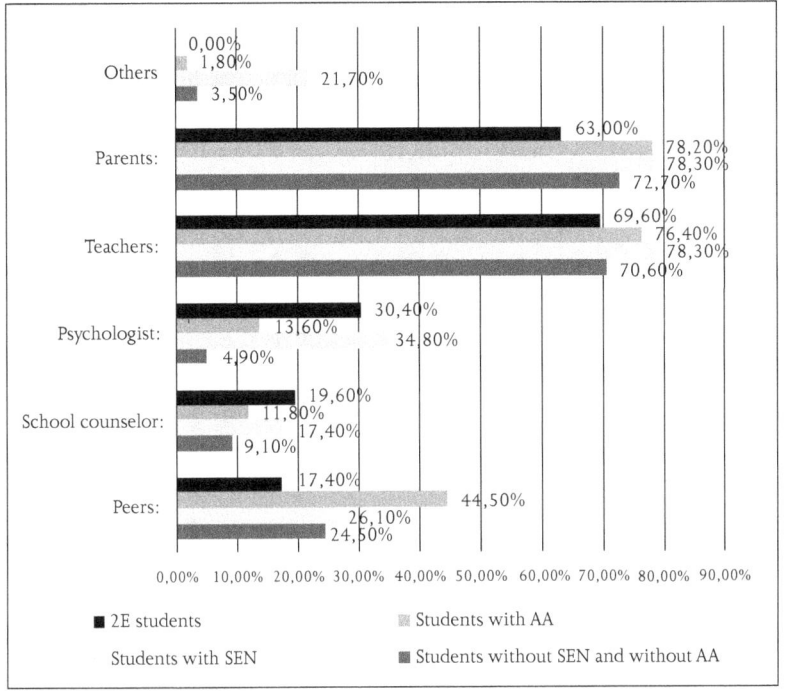

**Figure 3.3** Distribution of nominations by student group

declared by students with SEN and students with academic achievement. Interestingly, those with SEN (34.8%) and twice-exceptional students (30.4%) were more likely to report nominations by psychologists compared to the other groups. Declarations about nominations by psychologists showed clear differences between groups, $\chi^2(3) = 28.98$, p $< 0.001$. The respondents' answers indicated that the fewest nominations came from school educators (the chi-squared test revealed no significant differences between groups, $\chi^2(3) = 4.24$, p $= 0.237$). To conclude, twice-exceptional students represented the group least likely to report experiencing nominations from parents and teachers compared to the other groups of students highlighted in the study, while also reporting nominations from school psychologists and educators less frequently than students with SEN. This may be due to the problems described earlier related to the lack of knowledge about the phenomenon of twice-exceptionality among parents and professionals, or to the masking of giftedness by special educational needs (Baldwin et al., 2015).

### Perception of the Respondents as a Gifted Person

An interesting topic involves differences in respondents' self-perceptions. Respondents were asked to answer the question, "Do you consider yourself a gifted person?" Twice-exceptional students were least likely to perceive themselves as gifted (17.4%), whereas academically successful students were most likely to do so (44.5%). Among students claiming to have SEN, 26.1% described themselves as gifted, and among students with no academic achievements and no SEN it was 24.5%.

These results suggest that despite objective academic achievement, twice-exceptional individuals may rate their potential lower. In addition, the difference in the results of the large number of statements about past appointments and the results of respondents' perceptions of themselves as gifted may be due to the attitude of adults about giftedness. Adults often tend to believe that giftedness in adulthood can only be mentioned when someone has significant achievements or awards. In a study by Perrone et al. (2007), participants defined "giftedness" in different ways, but most often as knowledge or performance well above average and the ability to learn quickly. The results indicate the need to educate and help gifted adults address misconceptions about their own abilities.

### Assessing One's Own Giftedness Using Silverman's Adult Giftedness Scale and the Ksiazak Adult Giftedness Scale

Beyond indicating whether respondents consider themselves gifted, participants completed two scales to assess their perceptions of giftedness and ability. Silverman's Adult Giftedness Scale (AGS) comprises 38 items that identify characteristics of giftedness (Silverman, 2005, 2009). On a 5-point Likert scale (ranging from "not at all" to "very true"), respondents rated the extent to which each characteristic describes them. Despite lacking a solid theoretical basis, the tool reported a Cronbach's reliability coefficient of 0.88 (Perrone et al., 2007). The Ksiazak Adult Giftedness Scale (KAGS, Ksiazak, 2010), on the other hand, contains 23 self-report questions based on Dabrowski's theory of hyperactivity and the three-ring conception of giftedness. The KAGS questions are answered on a 7-point scale. While demonstrating satisfactory internal consistency, the KAGS raises questions about relevance due to item redundancy (Jiménez-Soto et al., 2024). The results are presented in Table 3.2.

Table 3.2 Assessment of own abilities as measured by the AGS and KAGS Scales among students

| | Group | n | M | SD | F(3,318) | p | $\eta^2$ | Paired comparisons | | | |
|---|---|---|---|---|---|---|---|---|---|---|---|
| | | | | | | | | 1 | 2 | 3 | 4 |
| KAGS | Twice-exceptional students | 46 | 4.66 | 0.67 | 8.226 | <0.001 | 0.07 | — | | | |
| | Students with AA | 110 | 4.72 | 0.70 | | | | 0.961 | — | | |
| | Students with SEN | 23 | 4.53 | 0.61 | | | | 0.852 | 0.582 | — | |
| | Students without SEN and AA | 143 | 4.34 | 0.57 | | | | 0.014 | <0.001 | 0.517 | — |
| AGS | Twice-exceptional students | 46 | 3.65 | 0.36 | 43.466 | <0.001 | 0.29 | — | | | |
| | Students with AA | 110 | 3.81 | 0.30 | | | | 0.063 | — | | |
| | Students with SEN | 23 | 3.42 | 0.25 | | | | 0.015 | <0.001 | — | |
| | Students without SEN and AA | 143 | 3.40 | 0.27 | | | | <0.001 | <0.001 | 1.000 | — |

Note. n = number of observations; M = mean; SD = standard deviation; F = value of test statistic; p = statistical significance; $\eta^2$ = effect size.

The analyses conducted confirmed that students rated their abilities differently and that the resulting effect explained 7% of the variability in ability scores measured by the KAGS test. Analysis of paired comparisons using multiple testing showed that students with academic achievements and 2e students demonstrated significantly higher ability scores than students without SEN and without achievements. The group of students with SEN, despite non-significant results, tended to have lower ability scores compared to students with academic achievement and 2e students.

However, significant differences were found when assessing ability with the AGS, indicating moderate self-assessment of ability by the twice-exceptional students compared to the other groups. Students with academic achievements rated themselves highest, showing significantly higher scores than students with SEN and those from the no SEN and no achievements group, as well as biased differences compared to the twice-exceptional students. In contrast, students declaring no achievements showed no significant differences in the subjective assessment of their ability, regardless of whether they had SEN or not. This effect explained 29% of the variation in the subjective assessment of their own ability, indicating very high variability between groups in this regard.

### Subjective Well-Being and Global Life Satisfaction

The Personal Wellbeing Index (PWI), a tool to assess subjective well-being and global life satisfaction, was used to measure well-being. The PWI consists of seven items assessing different spheres of life, with the key factors being socio-economic status, social relationships, health and personal achievement. The tool showed good internal consistency and factor structure across studies (Khor et al., 2020). A one-factor analysis of variance was conducted in order to estimate the variation in global life satisfaction and well-being across student groups. Life satisfaction was measured by a single question derived from the PWI scale, according to the key, while well-being resulted from the sum of the other items from this tool. The analysis is presented in Table 3.3.

When analysing the results obtained, it was found that the students did not show a statistically significant difference in terms of global life satisfaction. The effect obtained accounted for only 2% of the variance, indicating little difference between the groups. For the level of

**Table 3.3** Well-being variation among students

| Variable | Group | n | M | SD | F(3,318) | p | $\eta^2$ | Paired comparisons | | | |
|---|---|---|---|---|---|---|---|---|---|---|---|
| | | | | | | | | 1 | 2 | 3 | 4 |
| Global life satisfaction | Twice-exceptional students | 46 | 6.00 | 2.26 | 2.151 | 0.100 | 0.02 | — | | | |
| | Students with AA | 110 | 6.67 | 1.88 | | | | 0.211 | — | | |
| | Students with SEN | 23 | 5.83 | 1.67 | | | | 0.986 | 0.240 | — | |
| | Students without SEN and AA | 143 | 6.47 | 1.97 | | | | 0.497 | 0.846 | 0.467 | — |
| Subjective well-being | Twice-exceptional students | 46 | 55.39 | 18.36 | 7.609 | <0.001 | 0.05 | — | | | |
| | Students with AA | 110 | 62.03 | 14.47 | | | | 0.070 | — | | |
| | Students with SEN | 23 | 48.99 | 12.20 | | | | 0.366 | 0.002 | — | |
| | Students without SEN and AA | 143 | 60.44 | 15.57 | | | | 0.218 | 0.847 | 0.006 | — |

Note. n = number of observations; M = mean; SD = standard deviation; F = value of test statistic; p = statistical significance; $\eta^2$ = effect size.

subjective well-being, significant variation was shown between groups, the effect was moderate and explained 5% of the variance of the variable. The highest levels of well-being were declared by students with academic achievement. Analysis of paired comparisons showed two statistically significant differences between students with SEN and students without SEN regardless of whether they had achievement or not. In both cases students with special educational needs had lower levels of well-being. Twice-exceptional students ranked between these groups; however, they did not differ significantly in their well-being evaluation.

## CONCLUSION

The findings presented in this chapter from a study that involved students who were entering higher education confirmed the existence of a significant group of twice-exceptional students, that is, individuals who achieve high academic results despite having special educational needs. Although this group was not the most numerous, the responses obtained showed that studnts with 2e evaluated their academic performance positively. In a study by Sandoval-Rodríguez and Conejeros-Solar (2024), 2e students gave similar positive feedback on the variety of study experiences, access to knowledge and expansion of self-awareness.

Twice-exceptional students, less frequently than other participants, experienced the perception of giftedness at earlier stages of education, not only by teachers but also by parents and peers. Simultaneously, they received less frequent nominations from psychologists or school educators than SEN students. This may stem from insufficient awareness in the educational system about this specific group and the difficulties of the simultaneous identification of both their strengths and limitations (Hill, 2020).

Twice-exceptional students were significantly less likely to identify themselves as gifted as compared to those with academic achievements. The results indicate that while psychologists recognized their potential, the twice-exceptional students themselves were more critical in assessing their abilities. This may be due to previous educational difficulties, a lack of adaptation of educational conditions or experiences related to their special educational needs (Lummiss, 2018). Consequently, despite objective academic achievements, such students may not fully recognize their potential, which may affect their further educational and professional development (Foley-Nicpon & Assouline, 2015).

Analysis of the results confirmed that there existed significant differences between twice-exceptional students and students with academic achievements on both the KAGS and AGS tests. Both groups of students scored higher on the KAGS compared to students without SEN and without achievements and students with SEN. Students with academic achievements rated their ability highest on both scales, while twice-exceptional students, despite their high scores on the KAGS, demonstrated a moderate self-assessment of ability on the AGS, suggesting a greater discrepancy in their perception of their own talents.

The lack of significant disparities in overall life satisfaction indicates that, despite their different burdens, twice-exceptional students do not rate their lives as less satisfying compared to other groups, which may suggest that they are able to adapt to challenges and gain satisfaction from academic success (Cotton et al., 2002; Trucchia et al., 2013). However, twice-exceptional students show lower levels of psychological well-being than students with academic achievements, while they do not differ significantly in this respect from students with SEN. This demonstrates the importance of addressing the specific psychological support needs of this group in order to minimize the negative effects related to their unique educational and life profiles.

**REFERENCES**

Aloka, P., Omare, J. M., Owuor, E. A., Okongo, C. & Owino, J. (2024). Well-being and mental health initiatives for students in universities. In *Mental health crisis in higher education* (pp. 1–13). IGI Global. https://doi.org/10.4018/979-8-3693-2833-0.ch001

Baldwin, L., Omdal, S.N. & Pereles, D.A. (2015). Beyond stereotypes. *TEACHING Exceptional Children*, 47, 216–225.

Barber, C. & Mueller, C.T. (2011). Social and Self-perceptions of adolescents identified as gifted, learning disabled, and twice-exceptional. *Roeper Review*, 33(2), 109–120. https://doi.org/10.1080/02783193.2011.554158

Bartnikowska, U. & Antoszewska, B. (2017). Children with special educational needs (SEN) in the Polish education system. *International Journal of Psycho-Educational Sciences*, 6(3).

Bellis M. A., Hughes, K., Jones, A., et al. (2013). Childhood happiness and violence: A retrospective study of their impacts on adult well-being. *BMJ Open*, 3, e003427. doi:10.1136/bmjopen-2013003427

Besnoy, K. D., Swoszowski, N. C., Newman, J. L., Floyd, A., Jones, P. & Byrne, C. (2015). The advocacy experiences of parents of elementary age, twice-exceptional children. *Gifted Child Quarterly*, 59(2), 108–123. https://doi.org/10.1177/0016986215569275

Bhat, H. N. & Bhardwaj, R. (2014). The concept of academic achievements. *International Journal of Education and Science Research Review*, 1(6), 93.

Cain, M., Kaboski, J. & Gilger, J. (2019). Profiles and academic trajectories of cognitively gifted children with autism spectrum disorder. *Autism*, 23, 1663–1674. https://doi.org/10.1177/1362361318804019.

Cohen, J. (2016). A power primer. In A. E. Kazdin (Ed.), *Methodological issues and strategies in clinical research* (4th ed., pp. 279–284). American Psychological Association. https://doi.org/10.1037/14805-018

Cotton, S. J., Dollard, M. F. & de Jonge, J. (2002). Stress and student job design: Satisfaction, well-being, and performance in university students. *International Journal of Stress Management*, 9, 147–162. http://dx.doi.org/10.1023/A:1015515714410

Donald, W. E. & Jackson, D. (2022). Subjective wellbeing among university students and recent graduates: Evidence from the United Kingdom. *International Journal of Environmental Research and Public Health*, 19(11), 6911. DOI:10.3390/ijerph19116911

Eloff, I., Mampane, M. R., Omidire, F., Ayob-Essop, S., Bester, S. & Kgopa, B. (2022). Dimensions of wellbeing of university students during a pandemic. *African Perspectives of Research in Teaching & Learning (APORTAL)*, 6(1).

Foley-Nicpon, M. & Assouline, S. G. (2015). Counseling considerations for the twice-exceptional client. *Journal of Counseling & Development*, 93(2), 202–211. https://doi.org/10.1002/j.1556-6676.2015.00196.x

Foryś, M. (2018). Diagnoza zdolności, uzdolnień, „podwójnej wyjątkowości" w działalności nauczyciela i specjalisty. *XXIV Konferencja Diagnostyki Edukacyjnej: Wspomaganie rozwoju kompetencji diagnostycznych nauczycieli*, Katowice. https://www.ptde.org/pluginfile.php/1378/mod_page/content/13/PTDE_2018_189.pdf

Freebern, G. (2023). Twice exceptional is a cruel double-edged sword. *ADDitude Magazine*, 25 April. https://www.additudemag.com/2e-adhd-autism-parent-child/

Garces, N., Fajardo, Z., Villao, M., Caguana, D. & Esteves, C. (2024). Relationships between mental well-being and academic performance in university students: A systematic review. *Salud, Ciencia y Tecnología – Serie de Conferencias*. https://doi.org/10.56294/sctconf2024972.

Hill, E. D. (2020). *Twice-exceptional college students narratives: When giftedness and mental health intersect* (Publication No. 3099) (Master's dissertation). University of North Dakota. https://commons.und.edu/theses/3099

Hossain, S., O'Neill, S. & Strnadová, I. (2023). What constitutes student well-being: A scoping review of students' perspectives. *Child Indicators Research*, 16(2), 447–483. https://doi.org/10.1007/s12187-022-09990-w

Jiménez, S., Navarro, R., Rubio, E., Ibáñez, M., Gutierrez, J. & Larrañaga, M. (2018). Health contributing factors in higher education students:

The importance of family and friends. *Healthcare*, 6(4), 147. https://doi.org/10.3390/healthcare6040147

Jiménez-Soto, A., Infante Rejano, E. & Scurtu Tura, M. C. (2024). *No gifted adult left behind: Validation and reliability of the Adultgiftedness Identification Screening Test (Agist)*. SSRN. https://papers.ssrn.com/sol3/papers.cfm?abstract_id=4988643

Johari, M. A. & Ahmad, S. (2019). Persepsi tekanan akademik dan kesejahteraan diri di dalam kalangan pelajar universiti di Serdang, Selangor. *EDUCATUM Journal of Social Sciences*, 5(1), 24–36. https://doi.org/10.37134/ejoss.vol5.1.4.2019

Khor, S., Cummins, R. A., Fuller-Tyszkiewicz, M., Capic, T., Jona, C., Olsson, C. A. & Hutchinson, D. (2020). Australian Unity Wellbeing Index – Report 36: Social connectedness and wellbeing. Australian Centre on Quality of Life, School of Psychology, Deakin University. http://www.acqol.com.au/projects#reports

Ksiazak, T.M. (2010). *Development of the Ksiazak Adult Giftedness Scale* (Unpublished).

Lo, C. C. & Yuen, M. (2015). Succeeding against the odds: Observations on coping by three intellectually very able university students with specific learning difficulties in Hong Kong. *Gifted Education International*, 1–16. https://doi.org/10.1177/0261429415585407

Lummiss, M. (2018). *Self-perceptions of twice-exceptional students: The influence of labels and educational placement on the self-concept of post-secondary G/LD students* (Master's dissertation). Ball State University.

Minnaert A. (2022). Inclusive support to safeguard the strengths of twice-exceptional students. *Madridge Journal of Behavioural and Social Sciences*, 5(1), 86–88. DOI:10.18689/mjbss-1000115

Mustafa, M. B., Rani, N. H. M., Bistaman, M. N., Salim, S. S. S., Ahmad, A., Zakaria, N. H. & Safian, N. A. A. (2020). The relationship between psychological well-being and university students academic achievement. *International Journal of Academic Research in Business and Social Sciences*, 10(7), 518–525.

Osamika, B., Lawal, T., Osamika, A., Hounhanou, A. & Laleye, M. (2021). Personality characteristics, psychological wellbeing and academic success among university students. *International Journal of Research in Education and Science*, 7(3), 805–821. https://doi.org/10.46328/IJRES.1898.

Perrone, K. M., Perrone, P. A., Ksiazak, T. M., Wright, S. L. & Jackson, Z. V. (2007). Self-perception of gifts and talents among adults in a longitudinal study of academically talented high-school graduates. *Roeper Review*, 29(4), 259–264. https://doi.org/10.1080/02783190709554420

Peters, D. (2015). The twice-exceptional adult: We often hear about "2e" children but what about adults? *Psychology Today*, 12 November. https://www.psychologytoday.com/intl/blog/worrier-warrior/201511/the-twice-exceptional-adult

Putri, T. & Novitasari, R. (2017). The relationship between peer attachment and psychological well-being of university students. *Psikologika Jurnal Pemikiran Dan Penelitian Psikologi*, 22(2), 101–116. https://doi.org/10.20885/psikologika.vol22.iss2.art8

Rodríguez, F., Espigares-López, I., Brown, T. & Pérez-Mármol, J. (2020). The relationship between psychological well-being and psychosocial factors in university students. *International Journal of Environmental Research and Public Health*, 17(13), 4778. https://doi.org/10.3390/ijerph17134778

Ronksley-Pavia, M. (2015). A model of twice-exceptionality. *Journal for the Education of the Gifted*, 38, 318–340. https://doi.org/10.1177/0162353215592499

Ronksley-Pavia, M., Grootenboer, P. & Pendergast, D. (2018). Privileging the voices of twiceexceptional children: An exploration of lived experiences and stigma narratives. *Journal for the Education of the Gifted*, 42(1), 4–34. https://doi.org/10.1177/0162353218816384

Rooij, E., Jansen, E. & Grift, W. (2018). First-year university students' academic success: The importance of academic adjustment. *European Journal of Psychology of Education*, 33, 749–767. https://doi.org/10.1007/S10212-017-0347-8

Sandoval-Rodríguez, K. & Conejeros-Solar, M. L. (2024). Voices of twice-exceptional students in their first year of higher education. *Gifted and Talented International*, 39(1), 60–69. https://doi.org/10.1080/15332276.2024.2340025

Sengil-Akar, S. & Akar, I. (2020). Academically gifted & albino: A narrative study of a twice-exceptional. *International Journal of Progressive Education*, 16(2), 279–296. https://doi.org/10.29329/ijpe.2020.241.19

Silverman, L. (2005). Are you an unrecognized gifted adult? Giftedness in Adults Rating Scale. https://static1.squarespace.com/static/5ec9e1a3d3815c7ebcd0503a/t/609c9ef92b17935c41820315/1744041662978/Giftedness+in+Adults+Scale.pdf

Silverman, L. (2009). The measurement of giftedness. In L. V. Shavinina (Ed.), *International handbook on giftedness* (pp. 947–970). Springer. https://doi.org/10.1007/978-1-4020-6162-2_48

Smyth, K. H. (2017). *Success of twice-exceptional college students screened by ACT versus SAT scores and major declaration in line with academic strength* (Doctoral dissertation). University of Tennessee: TRACE – Tennessee Research and Creative Exchange. https://trace.tennessee.edu/utk_graddiss/4654

Spicer, C. D. (2011). The emotional toll of being a twice-exceptional adult: A case study. In C. Wormald & W. Vialle (Eds.), *Dual exceptionality* (pp. 30–36). Australian Association for the Education of the Gifted and Talented.

Thorsteinsen, K. & Vittersø, J. (2018). Striving for wellbeing: The different roles of hedonia and eudaimonia in goal pursuit and goal achievement. *International Journal of Wellbeing*, 8(2), 89–109. DOI:10.5502/ijw.v8i2.733

Trucchia, S. M., Lucchese, M. S., Enders, J. E. & Fernández, A. R. (2013). Relationship between academic performance, psychological well-being, and coping strategies in medical students. *Revista de la Facultad de Ciencias Medicas (Cordoba, Argentina)*, 70(3), 144–152.

Willings, D. (1985). The specific needs of adults who are gifted. *Roeper Review*, 8(1), 35–38.

Wood, S. & Estrada-Hernández, N. (2009). Psychosocial characteristics of twice-exceptional individuals: Implications for rehabilitation practice. *Journal of Applied Rehabilitation Counseling*, 40(3), 11–20. https://doi.org/10.1891/0047-2220.40.3.11

World Health Organization. (2001). *Strengthening mental health promotion: Fact sheet No. 220.* World Health Organization.

Yu, L., Shek, D. & Zhu, X. (2018). The influence of personal well-being on learning achievement in university students over time: Mediating or moderating effects of internal and external university engagement. *Frontiers in Psychology, 8.* https://doi.org/10.3389/fpsyg.2017.02287

Migrant Students in Higher Education – Chances and Obstacles to Successful Achievement

# Four

## INTRODUCTION

The concept of migration includes the movement of individuals between areas that are distant from their previous place of residence with the aim of settling there for various periods of time (short, medium and long term). Given the subject of the analysis, the chapter includes selected aspects of the experience of individuals facing external migration, which means moving between different countries to settle in the territory of a country of which the individual is not a citizen. Such a decision can be motivated by various factors, including economic issues, aspirations to improve cultural capital (in individuals migrating for education) and family-related factors (joining a family member living in another country). However, in the case of refugeeism, the motive is associated with leaving the country of which the individual is a citizen for fear of persecution.

According to the World Migration Report (2024), international migrants accounted for 3.6% of the world's population in 2024. Compared to 2020 (2.8%), a noticeable upward trend was found. Also, a significant increase in the number of individuals in a refugee situation was reported between 2020 and 2024 (14 million people in 2020 compared to 35.4 million people in 2024). Part of the migrant population consists of young adults undertaking higher educational activities in the host country. Considering the opportunities for higher education, those in refugee situations and asylum seekers are at a particular disadvantage. According to UNESCO data, only about 5% of refugees undertook higher education in 2020, compared to the share of the general population in higher education (40%). However, these figures are vague, as universities do not always provide accurate data on the formal status of foreign students (mainly due to privacy issues) and provide reports on the number of international students in general (UNESCO, 2022).

DOI: 10.4324/9781003571674-4

Considering events such as the Arab Spring, the global economic crisis (2007–2008) and the attack of the Russian Federation on the eastern areas of Ukraine, which resulted in increased dynamics of migration, Castles et al. (2024) indicated the general trends of migration processes. In addition to globalization, they discussed changes related to the following aspects: 1) the direction of migration (the increase in significance of Europe as a migration destination); 2) the diversification of migrant populations in destination countries (co-occurrence of economic migrants, educational migrants and refugees); 3) the change of status from a country where emigration processes were predominant to a country where immigration became dominant (e.g. Poland); 4) the feminization of economic migration; and 5) the increase in the political status of migration when the issues involved require both national and global political decisions (Castles et al., 2024). The population of migrants in Poland is characterized by a relatively high level of human and cultural capital (taking education as its indicator). The citizens of Ukraine are the predominant group of migrants in Poland.

Data from the PESEL system (Duszczyk & Kaczmarczyk, 2022) indicated that the population was dominated by young individuals (47% < 18 years of age), followed by people of working age (46%) and seniors (7%). The population was feminized (women accounted for 42% of the working-age population) (Duszczyk & Kaczmarczyk, 2022).

Poland is not the most frequent destination country for migrants. However, the number of young adult foreigners undertaking studies in Poland has recently steadily increased. According to the Statistics Poland (2024), 107,100 foreigners studied in Poland in the 2023/2024 academic year. These were mainly individuals from Ukraine (43.1%), Belarus (11.8%) and Turkey (4.4%). According to the National Information Processing Institute (Radon, Foreign Students, 2023), next to the citizens of the above countries, individuals from Zimbabwe, Azerbaijan, Uzbekistan, China, Kazakhstan and Nigeria also studied in Poland in 2022. A noticeable upward trend was found in the selection of Polish universities by young adults from abroad (78,374 international students studied in Poland in 2019 [Radon, Foreign Students, 2023] and a 27% increase in the 2023/2024 academic year). International students mainly chose full-time studies (89,769 students in 2023 compared to 13,914 students in part-time studies). Students more often chose studies at private universities compared to state universities. Considering geographical distribution, the largest number of international students chose universities in the Mazovian Province (including Warsaw, the capital of Poland) (Radon, Foreign Students, 2023).

## CONSIDERING MIGRANT STUDENTS AS A TWICE-EXCEPTIONAL VULNERABLE GROUP

The subject of the analysis was the complex context of young adult migrant participation in educational university activities. It is characterized by the risk factors of failure and the opportunity for success. It was assumed that their situation was similar to the way the concept of twice-exceptionality is understood. They are not twice-exceptional individuals in the typical understanding of the term – i.e. combining an attribute of disability, the impaired function adversely affecting the ability to learn and perform daily social roles, with achieving success in a specific area of functioning (educational domain) – as it is presented in Chapter 1. However, since migration implies the need to adapt to new social and cultural conditions, components of the migrant experience include the following:

- separation from loved ones and the previous living environment (local environment, work, education);
- being in new cultural conditions that are different from previous socialization experiences;
- lack of knowledge (or poor knowledge) of the language of the host country;
- uncertainty about future living conditions (gaining access to resources such as income and housing);
- the risk of experiencing discrimination, stigmatization and social marginalization.

In addition, forced refugee migration is associated with a higher risk of exposure to traumatizing events compared to the general population, which is a risk factor for anxiety disorders and post-traumatic stress disorder (PTSD).

It can be considered that the stories of individuals in a migrant situation who achieve educational success (e.g. completing further stages of education, passing exams) or professional success (seen as active participation in the public, non-governmental sphere) in the host country are in the domain of interest of research on twice-exceptionality. Their vulnerability could be seen as comparable to a disability. The authors of the UNESCO report (2022) considered a specific category of "vulnerable migrants". Similarly, according to Mihut (2024, p. 16), students with migrant experiences constituted one of the vulnerable groups in academic settings. Cantat et al. (2024) indicate the similarity of status in the academic domain of young adults in a refugee situation and students with disabilities, with low stratification being the representatives of discriminated ethnic groups and women given the historical context.

In turn, Erisman and Looney (2007), Szelényi and Chang (2002) and Soria and Stebleton (2013) put forward the thesis that the experiences of migrant students differed from the academic experiences of young adults studying in native settings, which warrants further research on the specificity of social, pedagogical and psychological phenomena that characterize the context of migrant participation in academic domains. Santinho and Rebelo (2024) assumed that many factors limiting the possibility of succeeding in educational goals were determined by the status of migrants and representatives of other underprivileged social groups. These included limited access to resources to meet basic needs (e.g. renting a house, access to medical care), restricted access to the employment market, interrupted education and experiencing various forms of violence both systemic and interpersonal). In addition, individuals in a situation of migration experience difficulties due to poor knowledge of the language of the host country.

Rückert (2015) found that students in a migrant situation experienced the same difficulties as the citizens of the country. Additionally, compared to native students, they experienced higher exposure to stressors resulting from a deficit of support from loved ones, the need to adapt to new social and cultural conditions, including belonging to a new educational system, which could violate a sense of security, but could also create the need to change their definition of identity (e.g. students may experience frustration at educational failure if they were successful in their country of origin).

According to Rückert, experiencing culture shock, communication problems and loneliness, and experiencing social isolation and concerns about one's own social well-being increase the risk of mental health disorders.

### Dimensions of Vulnerability in Migration Contexts

As indicated above, vulnerability is one of the terms used to describe the status of individuals in a situation of migration, especially of a refugee status related to seeking asylum and the need to leave their home countries due to armed conflict. Reviewing the definitions of the term in the social sciences discipline, Gilodi et al. (2024) found that vulnerability was expressed in the following ways:

- increased likelihood of exposure to risk factors (economic, health, relational, social) compared to the general population;
- limited capacity to obtain resources and cope with risk factors;
- being in a disadvantaged social position, which is expressed in reduced decision-making and dependence on the decisions of others with exposure to experiencing discrimination and violence (structural violence, hate crimes).

When analysing the situation of young adult migrants and their access to educational resources, it is essential to consider factors related to the following:

- innate vulnerability (individual's resilience, intrapersonal and interpersonal competencies and past experiences of coping with problematic situations are considered);
- situational vulnerability (individual's experiences of exposure to stress and potentially traumatizing events, access to resources, social security, controllability and decision-making are considered);
- structural vulnerability (the formal status of individuals as representatives of a particular social category, the risk of marginalization, discrimination and deficits in systemic protection from abuse are considered).

Given the above analyses, it can be considered that migrants are a vulnerable group, prone to experiencing social marginalization, expressed in incomplete and significantly worse access to resources (e.g. work, social factors, security, decision-making) compared to representatives of groups with similar social placement (cf. Murdoch et al., 2016). They constitute a homogenous social category. Different types are distinguished considering the variables such as the main motive for migration (economic, educational, fear for safety), the decisiveness of migration undertaking (a decision made independently or by another person, such as parents) and belonging to the first or second generation of migrants. They differ in terms of migration expectations and goals, sense of control over events and experienced risks to bio-psycho-social wellbeing. Research on migration issues requires the adoption of an interdisciplinary perspective and the intersectional location of related issues (such as the migrant's ethnic identity, gender and stratification location). The types of migration include internal and international, temporary and permanent, and regular and irregular migrations. However, the population included in the different types of migrants can dynamically change their status. Individuals who decided to migrate temporarily related to their studies can move into permanent migrant status, taking a decision to stay longer in the host country (King, 2012)

In turn, due to migration that is part of personal stories, the following can be distinguished in the general student population: 1) students who constitute the second generation of migrants (studies in Germany indicated their lower participation in secondary education preparing them for higher education, followed by lower participation in higher education); and 2) international students, including two subcategories: a) those who have come to a country of which they are not citizens to enter or continue their studies and have a legalized status, and may not define their own identity in terms of migration and related problems, and (b) refugees and asylum seekers (Wolter, 2020).

### EDUCATIONAL SUCCESS – SELECTED INDICATORS

Discussing the opportunities and limitations associated with achieving educational success of representatives of a specific group of society, it is necessary to analyse relevant concepts and identify the main indicators of the phenomenon. Educational success can be understood by referring to various indicators, depending on the adopted theoretical basis (structural and functional, emancipatory/counter-hegemonic, phenomenological).

### Structural-Functional Indicators of Success

From the structural-functional perspective, which refers to the meritocratic norm, objective and measurable achievements of students expressed by their educational results (test scores, credits) and the occurrence of other academic achievements (e.g. publication of scientific papers) are treated as the priority in identifying success. This approach can correspond to the concept of adequate classes involved in academic activities, which results in positive final scores. Additionally, the individual attends such classes and participates in additional activities (e.g. research projects and scientific conferences).

Another indicator is associated with undertaking employment in a profession related to the studied discipline or the wish to undertake such a job in the future. The final group of indicators is connected with the social aspect linked to involvement in academic organizations (e.g. scientific circles) and activities undertaken in the local environment (e.g. volunteering related to the studies, activity for the emancipation of other representatives of minority groups). The subjective indicator (referring to the theoretical phenomenological perspective of the lived world) is the sense of self-efficacy (Weathertone & Schussler, 2021).

### Counter-Hegemonic and Emancipatory Perspectives

In turn, as regards the counter-hegemonic emancipatory perspective, success is determined by the social advancement of representatives of underprivileged groups and the crossing of barriers determined by structural and cultural factors (related to the social meaning attributed to ethnic characteristics, gender or class identity). Indicators of success in such an approach can include the mere fact of entering and continuing studies regardless of the results and achieving a level of education higher than that of one's parents or rare for representatives of a particular social group (e.g. people in a refugee situation and asylum seekers).

Weathertone and Schussler (2021) found that it was necessary to consider hegemony theory and critical race theory in research on educational success achieved by representatives of different social groups.

### Phenomenological Perspectives and Lived Experience

As regards the phenomenological perspective of the lived world, success can be understood as psychological well-being associated with participation in the structures of higher education, a sense of belonging to related social groups, as an experience of individual development (associated with expanding knowledge of the study area, acquiring cultural competence of the host country) and experiencing satisfaction (cf. Weathertone & Schussler, 2021).

### Research on First-Generation and Underprivileged Students

O'Shea and Delahunty (2018) reported the results of a study on the indicators of academic success achieved by first-in-family students. Furthermore, some of them represented the characteristics of underprivileged social categories expressed by such indicators as low socioeconomic status (50%), disability (4%), belonging to ethnic minorities (3%) and having a refugee status (2%). The respondents and informants in the qualitative part of the research interpreted success as a state seen in obtaining positive feedback from academics, gaining progress in acquiring competencies associated with studies, satisfaction with the ability to continue studies, realizing a goal that seemed impossible to achieve, developing resilience, completing higher education and obtaining a professional title. Experiencing success was also described by the representatives of the research sample as a feeling of joy, happiness, satisfaction, pursuing a passionate activity and obtaining qualifications for a profession that was a source of satisfaction. The respondents also expressed the opinion that the mere fact of undertaking studies and continuing them was a success despite the difficulties related to the need to function in other social roles (employee, parent).

### Structural and Cultural Dimensions of Academic Success

Oh and Kim (2015) focused on understanding academic success from the structural and cultural dimensions. As regards the former, they distinguished between two theoretical dimensions: a structural dimension aimed at the race, and one focused on the class. To explain the opportunities and limitations associated with reaching success, the representatives of the racial dimension considered factors related to the meaning associated with identity factors (such as ethnicity), which could limit the chances of gaining access to resources due to discriminatory practices. From this perspective, stereotypes related to ethnic or class characteristics and related discrimination were understood as the basis for structural constraints to access value resources, including those related to higher education and success-related factors within it. The representatives of the class perspective argued that opportunities to access resources and achieve success were determined by the socioeconomic status. Analysing the opportunities to access resources of the representatives of migrant populations, Oh and Kim indicated a third group of factors, which were defined as structural group-specific factors. They included premigration variables (educational status and access to it in the migrant's country of origin, the cultural capital of the migrant at the time of arrival in the host country and educational aspirations within its structure).

However, from the perspective of cultural theories, the chances of accessing and succeeding in higher education result from the cultural orientation toward education in the migrant environment of origin (the dominant cultural pattern in society, patterns typical of ethnic groups and status patterns), the placement of education in the structure of culturally recognized values and the relationship between the value attributed to education and another participation of the individual (e.g. obligations to the family).

Sen (1993) contrasted the neoliberal conception of success based on quantitative indicators of the capability approach with conception related to qualitative factors, such as valuable social functioning that results in achieving outcomes valued by the individual.

## CHANCES AND OBSTACLES OF ACHIEVEMENT OF EDUCATIONAL SUCCESS

The chances of educational success for young adult migrants are determined by many factors, including systemic (political, legal, university regulations), cultural, social, economic and individual ones.

Within the categories, the following factors are considered in the analysis of chances of successful achievement: 1) inclusiveness vs. exclusiveness of the educational system; 2) communicative competence of students; 3) their cultural flexibility; 4) their position in social networks; 5) resilience to stressors; and 6) access to resources (labour market, housing).

### Stress Factors Among International Students

Amanvermez et al. (2023) conducted a study on a sample of 2,196 students in the Netherlands, of whom 556 (25.67%) were international students (mainly from Europe [74.18%], including Germany, the UK and Greece, and the Asia-Pacific region [8.8%]). They showed a higher level of declared stress among international students compared to native students.

The main sources of stress were life in general, financial issues, concerns about the health of loved ones, relationships with people at university and work, problems of others, family relationships and concerns related to romantic and intimate factors. Compared to native students, they declared less concern about their health. Factors such as stress related to financial situation, health of loved ones and life in general were statistically significantly related to the occurrence of depression and anxiety symptoms.

### Language Competence as a Critical Success Factor

The findings of a qualitative study by Kim (2012) on a sample of South Korean students in the United States of America found that language competence was the main source of difficulties for foreigners associated with studying. Working with foreign-language texts (textbooks, source texts) and preparing assignments in a foreign language required a significant amount of time and intellectual effort in such students.

Difficulties in formulating oral statements in class resulted in experiencing frustration and having a low status in the student group. The study respondents described their status as a "handicap" with which associated limitations must be accepted. The study respondents indicated the importance of relationships with academics, stressing the significance of their understanding of the specific situation and experiences of international students and the manifestation of supportive attitudes. Experiences concerning the attitudes of academics varied. The respondents indicated experiencing attention (e.g. thorough and accurate correction of assignments). They also expressed the opinion that lecturers ignored them during classes, paid more attention to native students and did not carefully control the process of competence acquisition by international students. Interactions with peers in the group of students representing the host society, belonging to the group of immigrants with a common national identity and representing the general group of international students were other essential factors regarding the adaptation process.

Cross-Cultural Educational Adaptation

Randall et al. (1998) conducted a study on 134 international students of Asian origin at the University of Ryukyus (Japan). The largest groups were: non-Chinese Asian group (39.5%), followed by China and Taiwan (33.6%), Latin America (13.4%), North America and Europe (7.5%) and those from Africa and the Middle East (5.2%). The respondents indicated the co-existence of educational migration with increased stress compared to its level experienced in the country of origin and the intensity of somatic symptoms (e.g. severe fatigue, gastrointestinal complaints, headaches, skin complaints, general feeling of being unwell). Among the stressors, 47.8% of respondents indicated a sense of loneliness caused by separation from loved ones (family, friends and work environment), followed by 41.1% of respondents indicating that the source of deterioration of well-being was associated with a less active social life, while 31.3% of respondents reported anxiety about their career after returning to their home country when they had not been able to achieve their academic aims while being in a foreign country.

On the other hand, factors limiting the chances of educational achievement included language problems (55.2%), inadequate reference material in the library and laboratories (34.3%), difficulty due to unfamiliarity with Japanese study methods (32.1%) and inadequate guidance from teachers and advisors (26.9%). Furthermore, 26.1% of the study subjects indicated inadequate academic background (social relations, social life).

Therefore, the main source of difficulties in the process of higher education of international students was related to language problems (due to insufficient knowledge of the language of the host country), followed by difficulties in adaptation to the cultural context based on different patterns (mainly concerning the implementation of the educational process) than those found in the migrant's country of origin. Furthermore, the difficulties were also associated with concerns about one's economic well-being (ability to meet material needs), concerns about the well-being of relatives who stayed in the country of origin and concerns about the development of one's career after returning to their native country.

### Unique Challenges of Refugee and Asylum-Seeking Students

A specific group of migrants are individuals who left the country of their citizenship due to armed conflicts in its territory, refugees and asylum seekers. This is the part of the migrant population that presents with a higher risk of exposure to potentially traumatizing situations compared to the general population. Their stories are associated with specific stages of refugee existence – the phase preceding the decision to leave the homeland due to risks to the safety of themselves and their loved ones, the phase of refugee migration characterized by risk factors and the phase of temporary or permanent settlement in the host country.

Based on a study of a sample of Ukrainian migrants residing in the United States, Andrushko and Lanza (2024) found that 76% of respondents described their own experience of forced migration as traumatic, 61% reported avoiding thoughts, emotions and feelings about the war in their homeland, 46% indicated struggling with thoughts of guilt and self-blame for not being in Ukraine and 8% were unable to define their feelings. As the most difficult parts of the experience related to their stay abroad, the respondents indicated distance from home and family (47%), language difficulties (40%) and new culture (36%), while 22% of the respondents indicated all of the above.

The risk of PTSD in the migrant population with refugee experiences was higher (8–10%) than in the general population (3.5%, according to US data) (Fazel et al., 2005; IWOFR Conference, 2020).

Blackwell (1988) stressed that young adults who came from countries experiencing armed conflicts, or which had a regime or dictatorship and were politically involved in their country of origin could experience fears about their relatives (or others with whom they had social relations) in a situation of migration. The fears could be accompanied by experiencing a conflict of values resulting from the belief in the righteousness of one's actions, showing disobedience to the regime and the belief in protecting loved ones. In turn, when informed of the arrest, death or any form of violence against loved ones who had stayed in their country of origin, refugees could experience a sense of guilt stemming from the belief that it was caused by political retaliation, and could also experience the feeling of being ineffective in protecting their family, thus failing their loved ones.

## THE STATUS OF FOREIGN STUDENTS IN POLAND

Given the legal system allowing individuals to study in a situation of migration, it is formally inclusive in Poland. Studies can be undertaken regardless of age by a person who has a document confirming secondary or higher education that allows them to continue education at a certain level (first-cycle, second-cycle, or doctoral studies). In the case of candidates from countries that are signatories to the 1961 Hague Convention, the document confirming the completion of the stage of education allowing the individuals to study is confirmed by means of an apostille. For citizens of countries that have not signed the Hague Convention, its legalization is required. The document on which the candidate applies for admission to university must include the information that the document entitles the individual to pursue higher education in the country where it was issued. If such information is not included in the document, the candidate must obtain an additional certificate confirming that the credential (certificate, diploma) allows for higher education in the country in which it was issued. Such a certificate can be obtained from the educational authorities of the country where the document was issued, a consul of the Republic of Poland in the country whose educational authority issued the credential or from a diplomatic representative or a consular office of the country that issued the document and operates in Poland (Required documents, University of Silesia, n.d.).

A fee is charged to foreigners undertaking full-time studies in Poland at state universities. The following individuals are exempt from the fee in state universities: citizens of a European Union member state, Switzerland or a member state of the European Economic Area, individuals with a permanent residence permit in Poland, long-term residents of the European Union, individuals with a temporary residence permit in Poland, those with refugee status, the status of temporary protection or subsidiary protection in Poland, holders of the Card of the Pole or those who are ascendants, descendants or spouses of Polish citizens.

In addition, in the case of studies in Polish, candidates are required to have a certificate confirming their knowledge of the Polish language at least at the C1 level.

### Housing and Employment Challenges

Das and Kochaniewicz (2015) indicated the accommodation difficulties of international students in Poland (Poznań) who were not given a place in dormitories. The search for a flat in the rental market is hindered by international students' lack of knowledge or a poor knowledge of the Polish language, lack of knowledge or a poor knowledge of English in lessors and increasing rental prices when the lessee is a foreigner. In turn, limiting factors for labour activation include the lack of official approval for non-EU students who do not have a status that determines the right to undertake employment and the lack of sufficient knowledge of the Polish language at the level required by employers.

### Social Integration and Evolving Public Opinion on Refugees and Migrants

Another issue related to the social context conditioning adaptation of international students at Polish universities is their location in the structure of formal and informal social networks and the establishment of social ties in the environment of the host country. One of the factors determining such placement is related to the attitudes of Poles toward migrants. The results of public opinion polls indicate that the attitudes of tolerance toward individuals in a refugee situation have been steadily declining since 2015. In May 2015, 72% of respondents expressed the opinion that refugees should be accepted in Poland and should be given the opportunity to settle and should be accepted until there was an opportunity to return to their homeland. In turn, 21% of respondents believed that refugees should not be accepted in Poland (7% were undecided on this issue).

In January 2016, 41% of respondents showed a positive opinion toward accepting refugees, while 53% showed a negative opinion (CBOS, 2016, p. 2). The increase in negative attitudes toward migrants occurred during the intensification of the discourse of the populist Law and Justice party that was in power at the time, according to whom migrants were a source of sanitary hazard (disease carriers), threats to native culture and potential criminals (Cywiński et al., 2019; Troszyński & El-Ghamari, 2022). In October 2021, 42% of respondents believed that Poland should accept refugees from countries experiencing armed conflict, while the opposite opinion was declared by 48% of respondents (CBOS, 2021). In April 2022, after the full-scale attack by the Russian Federation on Ukraine, 91% of respondents expressed the opinion that Poland should accept Ukrainian refugees as a result of the armed conflict, while a negative opinion was expressed by 4% of the respondents (CBOS, 2022).

A study on a sample of 203 students of the pedagogical degree programme at the University of Bialystok in 2020 indicated that 44% of respondents declared a negative attitude toward the prospect of accepting refugees and asylum seekers in Poland, 46% declared an ambivalent attitude and only 10% expressed a positive attitude. Negative attitudes were based on: 1) arguments related to competition for limited economic and social resources related to access to the labour and housing markets; 2) arguments related to security concerns – Islam was stereotypically identified with violent practices; and 3) arguments associated with concerns about cultural and national identity, which could be changed by refugees and asylum seekers, as reported by the respondents (Danilewicz, 2020).

Indicators of attitudes toward representatives of minority groups (immigrants) include perceived similarity/difference toward them and social distance. As indicated previously, the citizens of Ukraine constitute the predominant group of immigrants in Poland.

Research findings from the field of social psychology presented by Bilewicz (2023) indicated that Poles perceived Ukrainians as similar or very similar to themselves (77% of respondents, N=673), or even identical to Poles (4%). The study also indicated the dominance of attitudes that allowed Ukrainian citizens to function in close social distance with the respondents in spaces such as work (94% of respondents) and neighbourhood (95%). The study was conducted shortly after the full-scale attack by the Russian Federation on Ukraine in 2022.

Another indicator of attitudes toward migrants is related to declared emotions toward this social group. Data presented by Karaś and Traczyk (2025), who represent the More in Common Foundation, showed that overall attitudes toward immigrants were neutral (on a scale of −50 to +50, the score was 0). However, considering the ethnic identity of individuals residing in or potentially arriving in Poland, the study indicated the predominance of cold feelings toward Muslims and ethnic groups generally defined as Arabs, while warm feelings were related to Ukrainians and the general category of refugees.

Another social component that determines the well-being of students is their placement in the cultural space of the host country, as well as their adaptive competence to new social and cultural conditions. From the functionalist perspective, adaptation understood in this way can be operationalized as the understanding of symbols, culture and history of society, as well as competence to apply knowledge under academic conditions, respect social norms, function in social roles and recognize values characteristic of the host group.

The process of adaptation involves four stages, including contact with the culture of the host society, learning about the requirements and constraints associated with it, developing responses and developing the competence to cope with obstacles (Kim, 2012). The similarity of cultural patterns acquired by migrants in the course of socialization to those predominant in the host society is a factor that improves adaptation to new conditions. As mentioned earlier, the citizens of Ukraine are a dominant group of immigrants. The similarity of language and cultural patterns (especially of those coming from its western parts) can be treated as a factor facilitating adaptation. Dolińska et al. (2024) indicated the results of a study that focused on the reasons for the choice of studies at two Polish state universities (the Maria-Curie Skłodowska University in Lublin and the University of Wroclaw) by the students at these universities in the 2022/2023 academic year who came from Ukraine, Belarus, Lithuania and Russia.

The respondents most often indicated that the following factors were motives for studying and choosing a university in Poland: the desire to work outside of one's homeland, knowledge of the Polish language or the similarity of the language to their native language, the relatively low cost of living in Poland, the perception of Poles as open to foreigners and the recognition that access to higher education in Poland was easier than in other countries. They also indicated the importance of cultural proximity and the desire to learn a new culture and language.

### Psychological Capital and Academic Success

The attributes that constitute psychological capital determining the motivation to make an effort to study and perseverance are among the non-specific psychological factors in the research on the chances of successful academic achievement. Indicators of psychological capital included self-efficacy, hope, optimism and resilience. Self-efficacy was expressed by an individual's willingness to take on challenges, the belief that the individual could motivate themselves to act and has sufficient intellectual resources and competence to complete a task successfully under certain circumstances. It is a trait that is mainly analysed with reference to social-cognitive theory.

Hope is expressed by the co-occurrence of agency and planning to achieve a goal (pathways), a positive motivational state. On the other hand, optimism is a generalized positive tendency to anticipate future events and the using of the positive cognitive scripts of explaining events. It is a key trait for the occurrence and maintenance of expectations of success. Another trait that constitutes psychological capital is resilience. It is expressed by the ability to return to equilibrium when experiencing failure, and to flexibly develop new adaptive strategies that promote risk avoidance (Martínez et al., 2019). Martínez et al. (2019) indicated that psychological capital expressed by confidence in one's self-efficacy, hope for the positive development of events, optimistic anticipation of the future and resilience was conducive to the development of academic engagement. Indicators of engagement included vigour, dedication to activities and a sense of being absorbed in an activity (absorption). Vigour was expressed by the willingness to bear the effort and the ability to endure difficulties. It also covered energy involvement and maintaining mental efficiency while performing a task, feeling enthusiasm, a sense of meaning, satisfaction and pride in the task at hand.

Grabowska et al. (2023) conducted a study on a sample of 141 Ukrainian citizens residing in Poland, of whom 92% were women, 77% had higher education and 56% were economically active individuals. They showed that among those identifying themselves as war refugees, the indicators of mental capital (self-efficacy, optimism and hope) were weaker than in the group of those not considering themselves refugees. However, no difference was found as regards resilience. Most of the respondents (94%) defining themselves as war refugees declared that they thought about war at least once a day and indicated pain and grief as predominant feelings (85%). A positive correlation was noted between sustaining social relations and social support and the psycho-physical condition of those who defined themselves as refugees (from the formal point of view, they are mostly beneficiaries of temporary protection). Social relations and support were particularly important to resilience (Grabowska et al., 2023).

**CONCLUSIONS**

Based on the analysis, several conclusions can be drawn. They are enumerated as follows.

1. Educational success analysed from the perspective of different theoretical approaches is based on diverse indicators, implying the understanding of this phenomenon as the achievement of objective, systemically recognized achievements, as well as the transcending of stratification barriers by individuals representing socially disadvantaged groups, and as the general well-being and satisfaction of the student in functioning in the academic role, acquiring knowledge and gaining the possibility to perform the preferred profession.

2. The chances and obstacles of educational success for young adult migrants are diverse. They are related to both systemic and structural factors (inclusive vs exclusive nature of the university, access to basic social resources, the scholarship system, access to the labour market), as well as to the social climate related to those in the migration situation (which consists of the structure of social attitudes) and the cultural and psychological capital of the student (language competence, cultural competence, resilience, access to the social support system and the sense of security related to the family situation).
3. The situation of young adults entering, continuing and successfully completing higher education who are in the situation of forced migration (especially refugees and asylum seekers) and young adults who form the second generation of migrants can be regarded as having the characteristics of twice-exceptionality. Compared to the general population, they are under-represented in the structure of students of host countries with a vulnerable status expressed through an increased probability of experiencing risks (structural, social, mental health) and increased exposure to traumatizing events at different stages of their lives. They are also exposed to experiencing structural violence and restrictions on access to resources, and some of them achieve educational success despite confrontations with constraints.
4. The difficulties experienced by young adults undertaking higher education in the host country in the migration situation are specific and non-specific (related to factors that constitute barriers to success for the native young adult population as well).
5. The specific nature of difficulties and constraints in achieving educational success for young adults in the migration situation is related to separation from loved ones, a sense of lack of support from them, a sense of the weakening of previous social activity, a poor knowledge of the language of the host country, communication difficulties resulting from the previously mentioned reasons and the low cultural competence of the participants in the interaction, and the migrant's fear of disclosing information about their own (family, social) situation. These difficulties also include obstacles associated with access to housing, formal problems related to updating

documents that allow the continuation of stay in the host country, the nature of migration and social policies of individual countries, the cultural competence of professionals in the host country (students, lecturers, representatives of aid professions), the need to adapt to a new form of higher education, as well as concerns about confrontation with attitudes of intolerance toward the identity of "the Other", ethnically and culturally different in the social space in the host country.

6. Higher education is systemically placed in the context of the predominant structure of the historical narrative, socio-cultural imaginaries and political events. It is the context for the reproduction of knowledge and a potential space for the confrontation of identities representing the belonging to the space of centres, semi-peripheries and peripheries of globalization constructed based on colonial and post-colonial experiences and contemporary political events and processes. For this reason, universities and colleges have the responsibility to create constructive, dialogue-based and critical thinking-based civic spaces and to prepare graduates equipped with high cultural capital based on humanistic and interdisciplinary knowledge and cultural competencies conducive to the promotion of democratic ideas focused on values derived from humanitarianism and the concept of human rights.

7. Higher education is a source of individual and social capital from the perspective of the host country and the country of origin, to which some migrants return.

Recommendations for Effective Support Systems

Therefore, similar to the global nature of migration, young adult education is also part of strengthening global social and cultural capital. From the point of view of the needs of individuals in the migration situation, as well as considering the meso-social structure of study culture, and from the point of view of the aims of constructing a global space equipped with high-quality social and cultural capital, it is necessary to implement effective support. This should be based on cultural awareness and sensitivity for young adult migrants undertaking higher education in host countries. From the perspective of strengthening the chances of educational success for migrant students, the systemic support offered to them is important. It includes learning the language of the host country, and implementing advisor programmes and student support programmes.

The support can be related to diverse aspects of the functioning of young adults, such as issues associated with the preparation of documents required for legalization of residence and continuation of studies, assistance in gaining access to social resources (e.g. related to housing) and support in preparing to function in the professional field (e.g. through assistance in organizing mid-year internships). Other aspects are health support (including mental health, in which the cultural contexts of the students' country of origin are considered), emotional support, assistance in establishing social ties and being in networks of relationships (with other students, academics and entities from the local environment). As regards the implementation of such activities, it is important to consider the cultural context from which the student comes and the interaction patterns characteristic of the context, as well as the specificity of the social, cultural or political context that constitutes one of the motivating factors for leaving the country of origin.

## REFERENCES

Amanvermez, Y., Karyotaki, E., Cuijpers, P., Ciharova, M., Bruffaerts, R., Kessler, R. C., Klein, A. M., Wiers, R. W. & de Wit, L. M. (2023). Sources of stress among domestic and international students: a cross-sectional study of university students in Amsterdam, The Netherlands. *Anxiety, Stress, & Coping*, 37(4), 428–445. https://doi.org/10.1080/10615806.2023.2280701

Andrushko, Y. & Lanza, S. T. (2024). Exploring resilience and its determinants in the forced migration of ukrainian citizens: A psychological perspective. *International Journal of Environmental Research and Public Health*, 21(11), 1409. https://doi.org/10.3390/ijerph21111409

Bilewicz, M. (2023) Stosunek do imigrantów w Polsce. Konsekwencje kontaktu i mowy nienawiści. *Publikacje PAN*. https://publikacje.pan.pl/Content/127240/PDF/2023-01-DWUN-05.pdf [accessed 8 January 2025]

Blackwell, D. (1988) *Counselling and psychotherapy with refugees*. Jessica Kingsley Publishers.

Cantat, C., Cook, I. M. & Rajaram, P. K. (2024). Introduction: Opening up the university. In C. Cantat, I. M. Cook & P. K. Rajaram (Eds.), *Opening up the university: Teaching and learning with refugees* (Vol. 5, pp. 1–28). Berghahn Books. https://doi.org/10.2307/jj.14962379.5

Castles, S., de Haas, H. & Miller, M. J. (2024). *The age of migration. International population movement in the modern world* (5th ed.). Palgrave MacMillan.

CBOS. (2016). *Stosunek Polaków do przyjmowania uchodźców.* https://cbos.pl/SPISKOM.POL/2016/K_012_16.PDF [accessed 15 January 2025]

CBOS. (2021). *Opinia publiczna wobec uchodźców i sytuacji migrantów na granicy z Białorusią.* https://www.cbos.pl/SPISKOM.POL/2021/K_111_21.PDF [accessed 15 January 2025]

CBOS. (2022). *Polacy wobec uchodźców z Ukrainy.* https://www.cbos.pl/SPISKOM.POL/2022/K_062_22.PDF [accessed 15 January 2025]

Cywiński, P., Katner, F. & Ziółkowski, J. (2019) *Zarządzanie strachem. Jak prawica wygrywa debatę publiczną w Polsce?* Fundacja im. Stefana Batorego. https://www.batory.org.pl/upload/files/Programy%20operacyjne/Forum%20Idei/Zarzadzanie%20strachem.pdf [accessed 3 March 2025].

Danilewicz, W. (2020). Openness or prejudice? Students' attitudes to refugees in Poland. *Eastern European Journal of Transnational Relations*, 4(1), 135–149. DOI:10.15290/eejtr.2020.04.01.07

Das, S. & Kochaniewicz, A. (2015). Non-EU students' potential challenges in Poland: The case of the city of Poznan. *Trends Journal of Science Research*, 2(4), 117–120.

Dolińska, K., Jekaterynczuk, A., Makaro, J. & Podgórska, K. (2024). Motywacje studentów pochodzących z Europy Wschodniej do studiowania w Polsce – kontekst międzynarodowy, lokalny i instytucjonalny. *Edukacja Międzykulturowa*, 2(25), 114–133. DOI:10.15804/em.2024.02.08

Duszczyk, M. & Kaczmarczyk, P. (2022). The war in Ukraine and migration to Poland: Outlook and challenges. *Intereconomics*, 57(3), 164–170. DOI:10.1007/s10272-022-1053-6

Erisman, W. & Looney, S. (2007). *Opening the door to American dream: Increasing higher education access and success for immigrants.* Institute for Higher Education Policy.

Fazel, M., Wheeler, J. & Danesh J. (2005). Prevalence of serious mental disorder in 7000 refugees resettled in western countries: A systematic review. *Lancet*, 365(9467), 1309–1314. DOI:10.1016/S0140-6736(05)61027-6

Gilodi, A., Albert, I. & Nienaber, B. (2024). Vulnerability in the context of migration: A critical overview and a new conceptual model. *Human Arenas*, 7, 620–640.

Grabowska, I., Jastrzębowska, A. & Kyliushyk, I. (2023). Resilience embedded in psychological capital of Ukrainian refugees in Poland. *Migration Letters*, 20(3), 421–429. DOI:10.47059/ml.v20i3.2887

IWOFR Conference. (2020). *PTSD fakty i statystyki*, https://iwofr.org/pl/ptsd-fakty-i-statystyki/ [accessed 28 February 2025]

Karaś, U. & Traczyk, A. (2025). *Między niepokojem a życzliwością. Polki i Polacy wobec migracji.* Fundacja More in Common.

Kim, J. (2012) The birth of academic subalterns: How do foreign students embody the global hegemony of american universities? *Journal of Studies in International Education*, 12(6), 455–476, DOI:10.1177/1028315311407510

King, R. (2012). *Theories and typologies of migration: An overview and a primer.* Malmö Institute for Studies of Migration, Diversity and Welfare.

Makrooni, G. (2020). From challenge to empowerment: Cross-cultural experiences and perceptions of first-generation migrant family students. *Journal of Ethnic and Cultural Studies*, 7(3), 112–128.

Martínez, I. M., Youssef-Morgan, C. M., Chambel, M. J. & Marques-Pinto, A. (2019). Antecedents of academic performance of university students: Academic engagement and psychological capital resources. *Educational Psychology*, 39(8), 1047–1067. DOI: 10.1080/01443410.2019.1623382

Mihut, G. (2024). Learning from each other: Comparing the experiences of first-generation migrant, international and domestic students at Irish universities. *Journal of Studies in International Education*, 28(1).https://doi.org/10.1177/10283153221121397

Ministerstwo Nauki i Szkolnictwa Wyższego. (n.d.). Na jakich zasadach cudzoziemcy podejmują i odbywają nauki w polskich szkołach wyższych? https://www.gov.pl/web/nauka/na-jakich-zasadach-cudzoziemcy-podejmuja-i-odbywaja-nauki-w-polskich-szkolach-wyzszych [accessed 18 December 2024]

Murdoch, J., Guégnard, Ch., Griega, D., Koomen, M. & Imdorf, Ch. (2016). How do second-generation immigrant students access higher education? The importance of vocational routes to higher education in Switzerland, France and Germany. *Swiss Journal of Sociology*, 42(2), 245–263.

Oh, C. J. & Kim, N. Y. (2015). "Success is relative": Comparative social class and ethnic effects in an academic paradox. *Sociological Perspectives*, 59(2), 270–295.

O'Shea, S. & Delahunty, J. (2018). Getting through the day and still having a smile on my face! How do students define success in the university learning environment? *Higher Education Research and Development*, 37(5), 1062–1075.

Ośrodek Przetwarzania Informacji – Państwowy Instytut Badawczy. (2022). Foreigners at higher education institutions in Poland report 2022. https://radon.nauka.gov.pl/analizy/cudzoziemcy-na-uczelniach-w-Polsce-2022

Perales, F., Xiang, N., Hartley, L., Kubler, M. & Tomaszewski, W. (2022). Understanding access to higher education amongst humanitarian migrants: An analysis of Australian longitudinal survey data. *Higher Education*, 84, 373–397.

Picot, G. & Hou, F. (2018). Why immigrant background matters for university participation: A comparison of Switzerland and Canada. *International Migration Review*, 47(3), 612–642.

Radon, Foreign Students. (2023). https://radon.nauka.gov.pl/raporty/studenci_cudzoziemcy_2023 [accessed 6 December 2024]

Randall, M., Naka, K., Yamamoto, K., Nakamoto, H., Arakaki, H. & Ogura, C. (1998). Assessment of psychosocial stressors and maladjustment among foreign students of the University of the Ryukyus. *Psychiatry and Clinical Neuroscience*, 52, 289–298. DOI: 10.1046/j.1440-1819.1998.00396.x

Required documents, University of Silesia. (n.d.). https://us.edu.pl/kandydat/en/cudzoziemcy/wymagane-dokumenty/ [accessed 18 December 2024]

Rückert, H-W. (2015). Students' mental health and psychological counselling in Europe. *Mental Health & Prevention*, 3(1–2), 34–40.

Santinho, C. & Rebelo, D. (2024). Integrating refugees and migrants into higher education in Portugal? An action research experience. *Etnográfica*, 28(2), 431–450.

Sen, A. (1993). Capability and well-being. In M. Nussbaum & A. Sen (Eds.), *The quality of life* (pp. 9–30). Oxford University Press.

Soria, K. M. & Stebleton, M. (2013). Immigrant college students' academic obstacles. *Learning Assistance Review*, 18(1), 7–24.

Statistics Poland. (2024). Higher education in the 2023/2024 academic year – preliminary data. https://stat.gov.pl/en/topics/education/education/higher-education-in-the-202324-academic-year-preliminary-data,10,10.html [accessed 18 February 2025]

Szelényi, K., & Chang, J. C. (2002). ERIC review: Educating immigrants: The community college role. *Community College Review*, 30(2), 55–73.

Troszyński, M. & El-Ghamari, M. (2022). A great divide: Polish media discourse on migration, 2015–2018. *Humanities and Social Sciences Communication*, 9(27).

UNESCO. (2022). Higher education global data report. https://unesdoc.unesco.org/ark:/48223/pf0000389859 [accessed 17 February 2025]

Volkan, V. D. (2017). *Immigrants and refugees: Trauma, perennial mourning, prejudice, and border psychology* (1st ed.). Routledge.

Wallerstein, I. (2004). *World-systems analysis: An introduction*. Duke University Press.

Weathertone, M. & Schussler, E. E. (2021). Success for all: A call to re-examine how student success is defined in higher education. *CBE-Life Science Education*, 20(1).

Wolter, A. (2020). Migration and higher education in Germany. In M. Slowey, H. G. Schuetze & T. Zubrzycki (Eds.), *Inequality, innovation and reform in higher education*. Springer.

World Migration Report. (2024). Geneva, International Organization for Migration https://publications.iom.int/books/world-migration-report-2024

Blessed or Cursed? 2e Students Amidst the Meanders of Contemporary Mentality

# Five

## INTRODUCTION

Twice-exceptionality (2e) entails specific needs, challenges and risks, as discussed in earlier chapters. Here, we take a closer look at these dimensions through the lens of interactions between individuals and socio-cultural factors. Let us begin with the very foundation. The first quarter of our lives is a crucial period for the formation of our personality and identity. Our unique, genetically influenced characteristics confront environmental expectations, shaping the emerging self. As social beings, this process is influenced by both individual needs and those of surrounding social groups. When a child's autonomous needs are recognized, respected and met, a secure attachment style is more likely to form, leading to healthy development and a mature, flexible personality. Conversely, when emotional needs are neglected, the risk of long-term psychological and social harm increases significantly (Wojtyna & Gierczyk, 2025). It is easy to imagine that 2e individuals, with their numerous and specific needs, may be particularly vulnerable to neglect. As previously discussed, this includes the failure to recognize exceptional abilities that remain hidden behind disabilities, as well as the challenges associated with accurately diagnosing difficulties experienced by 2e individuals (see Chapter 1). Delayed identification of somatic or neurodevelopmental issues often leads to inappropriate criticism, limitations on developmental opportunities and – perhaps most significantly – a breakdown in the formation of an adequate self-concept.

Human development does not occur in a vacuum; it is shaped by factors related to the individual, their immediate social environment (family, close relationships, peer context) and broader systemic (e.g. educational systems) and cultural influences. Among the latter, several phenomena are particularly relevant to the experiences

DOI: 10.4324/9781003571674-5

of 2e individuals, and together constitute what has been termed the "right-thumb mentality" (Sikora & Górnik-Durose, 2013; Wojtyna & Gierczyk, 2025).

### RIGHT-THUMB MENTALITY AND THE REALITY OF 2E INDIVIDUALS

Contemporary individuals live in a culture that is heavily shaped by individualistic mentalities and promotes solutions that are clear-cut, evidence-based, fast, easy and preferably pleasurable. We seek modes of functioning that resemble the act of swiping a smartphone screen. We aim to simplify, to minimize discomfort and at the same time to achieve more, to see more, and to experience more – mediocrity is no longer enough.

The continuous advancement of technology and the broadly understood health and medical sciences enable us to overcome limitations that were once dictated by biology (such as disability, illness or ageing), economic status (as certain goods and services have become cheaper and more accessible) or geography (brought about by the ease of global communication). Easier access to information and insight into the lives of people from around the world increases our awareness of what is available – thus generating increasingly ambitious goals.

This desire to maximize one's aspirations is another feature of what Sikora and Górnik-Durose (2013) refer to as the right-thumb mentality. In our present-day reality, so much seems possible, yet it is easy to forget the limitations imposed by a 24-hour day or the biological constraints of our own bodies. The awareness that something theoretically attainable is slipping beyond our grasp gives rise to a strong sense of frustration.

### RIGHT-THUMB MENTALITY AND OVERDIAGNOSIS

The phenomena underlying the right-thumb mentality are also evident in the domains of health and well-being. According to the pathogenic paradigm, health is defined as the absence of disease. In contrast, the biopsychosocial paradigm encourages us to understand health as the pursuit of optimal physical, psychological, social and spiritual functioning. These two paradigms generate significant challenges for diagnostic processes – it is becoming increasingly difficult to delineate the boundary between health and illness, normality and disorder.

It is widely accepted that early identification of physical and/or mental health problems improves treatment effectiveness, mitigates negative consequences and generally supports better functioning. It is therefore no surprise that medicine continues to develop increasingly sensitive diagnostic methods. However, greater sensitivity does not automatically result in accurate diagnoses. Instead, it raises the risk of false positives, which leads to overdiagnosis.

Overdiagnosis is a particularly pressing issue in psychiatry. We are currently witnessing a phenomenon that Allen Frances (2013) termed a "diagnostic epidemic" – a dramatic increase in mental disorder diagnoses across the population, often without a proportional rise in the actual prevalence of serious cases. This trend is driven by broadened diagnostic criteria, over-identification and commercial pressures rather than by a real increase in morbidity. New editions of psychiatric classification manuals (DSM-5, ICD-11) introduce broader and more flexible criteria, which often result in the medicalization of normal psychological responses such as sadness, anxiety or rebelliousness. Difficulties with concentration may be hastily labelled as ADHD (attention deficit hyperactivity disorder), while someone who presents with unusual or "nerdy" behaviours may be prematurely diagnosed as autistic. Psychiatric evaluation lacks objective measures, making it especially prone to cognitive distortions and subjective interpretation. The absence of an absolute zero point in symptom severity assessment renders such evaluations inherently imprecise.

Modern individuals exhibit a strong tendency to reduce the discomfort associated with uncertainty. Consequently, in cases of diagnostic ambiguity, there is a clear bias towards either prematurely confirming or dismissing the presence of a disorder. The former often leads to a dismissal of genuine distress – a common experience for 2e individuals, particularly in earlier decades. The latter, on the other hand, may result in early access to support services, but also assigns individuals a diagnostic label that can shape how others perceive and interact with them.

As discussed in Chapters 1 and 2, such labelling carries consequences beyond the therapeutic context. A diagnosis may open the door to clinical and pharmacological treatment, including the use of psychostimulants. At present, there is significant and ongoing public debate about the overdiagnosis of ADHD and the corresponding overtreatment using methylphenidate. Concerns have been raised that some individuals exaggerate their symptoms and functional impairments in order to gain access to stimulant medications or to benefit from educational accommodations. In such cases, overdiagnosis contributes to growing social scepticism towards ADHD diagnoses, potentially discrediting the experiences of individuals who genuinely live with the condition. A similar situation is unfolding with the overdiagnosis of autism spectrum disorders (ASDs) – also commonly identified among 2e populations. In both cases, the overextension of diagnostic categories poses a risk not only to public trust but also to the accurate identification and support of those most in need.

## RIGHT-THUMB MENTALITY AND THE HEALTH AND WELL-BEING OF 2E INDIVIDUALS

Within the biopsychosocial framework of health, the right-thumb mentality – through its emphasis on maximizing outcomes – encourages behaviours aimed at eliminating every undesirable somatic symptom, even those with no clinical significance (e.g. purely aesthetic issues), as well as at fully developing all of one's capacities and abilities (Wojtyna & Stawiarska, 2013; Wojtyna & Gierczyk, 2025). This leads us into a trap of attempting to correct and optimize everything.

Meeting such expectations inevitably collides with real-life limitations and contributes to growing levels of chronic stress. Seemingly health-promoting behaviours begin to drift into pathology: physical activity turns into addiction; healthy eating morphs into orthorexia; preventive care becomes hypochondriac preoccupation. These tendencies no longer serve health or well-being.

Individuals within the 2e population may be particularly vulnerable to such risks (see Figure 5.1).

When a child is born with a disability, parents may seek to enhance their child's chances of success by attempting to correct perceived deficits. This may involve a high level of engagement in seeking specialist medical assistance, implementing increasingly advanced therapies and introducing rehabilitative and revalidation interventions aimed at compensating for the child's difficulties related to their disability. Frequently, this reflects an effort to transform disability into super-ability.

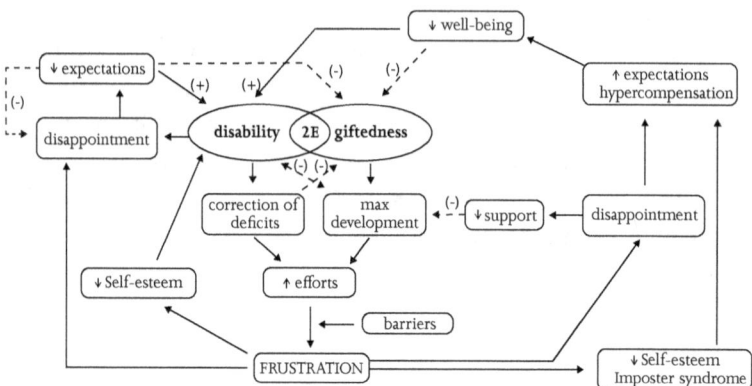

**Figure 5.1** The vicious circle associated with the "right-thumb" tendency to correct deficits and strive for full development

However, confrontation with real-world limitations – biological, economic, social – often leads to frustration. Not everything can be corrected, and focusing narrowly on a single area of functioning may inadvertently hinder development in other domains. For example, concentrating heavily on improving motor skills may impede a child's social development or the nurturing of their innate talents. This dynamic can result in low self-esteem, as well as disappointment – experienced both by caregivers and the child themselves. One possible way to alleviate this discomfort is to lower expectations, but such a strategy often leads to the perpetuation of disability-related challenges and limits the potential for the development of the child's gifts.

Conversely, the attempt to develop recognized talents – in the spirit of the right-thumb mentality – entails a compulsion to focus entirely on that goal. Letting the opportunity to reach one's full potential go to waste is seen as unacceptable. Yet even here, significant limitations may emerge, including those associated with disability. Frustration and disappointment may intensify. Previously available support is often reduced, thereby narrowing opportunities for growth. (We will return to this issue later.)

The right-thumb mindset promotes the belief that in today's world "everything is possible, as long as one tries hard enough". This frequently leads gifted individuals to engage in hypercompensation. In an effort to avoid disappointment, they invest even more energy into their pursuits—raising the bar ever higher in an attempt to prove their worth. From an outside perspective, such individuals may appear "high-functioning", and the emotional toll they pay can go unnoticed. Unfortunately, this intense commitment yields results only in the short term. In the long run, it depletes internal resources and significantly diminishes well-being. This, in turn, undermines the capacity to further develop one's talents and exacerbates difficulties related to disability.

When 2e individuals are identified at an early stage, they may receive strong environmental support from a young age to help nurture and strengthen their talents. Access to such specialized support can be highly beneficial; however, it is also important to acknowledge its potential downsides. A 2e individual may develop feelings of being an impostor, as their achievements may appear overshadowed by special treatment and granted privileges, which may undermine their self-esteem (Hutchins, 2015).

In Shytle's (2022) study of 2e adults, participants reported that despite having positive experiences in both their personal and professional lives, they often felt stagnation in their careers. They also expressed doubts about whether they were doing enough to realize their internal, value-driven generative goals. Impostor syndrome can lead to efforts to conceal perceived incompetence by withdrawing from opportunities to further one's achievements – whether in academic, professional or social domains (Hutchins & Rainbolt, 2017).

As illustrated in Figure 5.1, these inter-related mechanisms highlight the serious risk of disrupted self-esteem development in 2e individuals, and of exhausting one's internal resources on ineffective efforts – ultimately working against the very goals of supporting talent development and mitigating disability-related challenges.

### RISKS AND CONSEQUENCES OF NEGLECTING THE DEVELOPMENTAL NEEDS OF 2E INDIVIDUALS

The issues described above are relatively evident and fairly easy to identify. However, they often intersect with additional phenomena that may further hinder functioning and reduce the well-being of 2e individuals. The right-thumb mentality demands that no opportunity be wasted and that achievement be maximized. It also favours definitive, unambiguous solutions. In practice, this may translate into the promotion of educational and healthcare systems in which correcting deficits and developing talent become obligatory tasks, and failure to do so is seen as a serious form of neglect. Let us take a closer look.

Disability is defined in relation to the norms prevailing in a given social group. These norms are established based on various criteria – quantitative, socio-cultural or theoretical – and are often the subject of considerable controversy. Emotionally, however, disability is commonly associated with discomfort and negative connotations. It evokes uneasy reactions. In contrast, giftedness – though also a deviation from the norm—tends to evoke positive feelings and is generally welcomed.

The right-thumb mentality seeks to cultivate positive affect and minimize exposure to negative emotions. Thus, it is unsurprising that the impulse to support 2e individuals appears self-evident. Yet a fundamental issue arises: who defines their needs? Educational and healthcare systems are typically designed by individuals who have no personal experience of either twice-exceptionality or disability. As a result, there is a real risk that critical needs of 2e individuals will be overlooked – needs that these systems simply do not recognize or understand.

Let us return to the concept of the authentic self, one that integrates both autonomous inner needs and those arising from interaction with the social environment. Disability is an experience that alters the developmental trajectory of an individual, particularly when it is present from the earliest stages of life. In such cases, the person has no choice in the matter. Their developmental pathway diverges significantly from that of non-disabled individuals.

Disability becomes integrated into identity. One's perception and experience of reality develop differently; distinct competencies and coping mechanisms emerge. But does this "difference" necessarily imply inferiority?

The right-thumb mentality, in its pursuit of definitive and standardized solutions, tends to prompt efforts to correct difference in favour of a widely accepted "norm". However, an unreflective attempt to do so may result in a violation of the 2e individual's identity, undermining the possibility for the development of an authentic self. As noted in Chapter 6, one proposed solution to this problem is the inclusion of self-advocacy by people with disabilities, allowing for the negotiation and co-construction of the conditions under which they function within educational systems.

The situation with giftedness is somewhat different. While the right-thumb mentality similarly imposes a demand for heightened activity aimed at developing one's abilities, in practice, a gifted individual retains a degree of choice. They may choose to develop this aspect of their life, but they are not obligated to do so. They may follow a developmental path similar to that of non-gifted individuals, and this will not necessarily hinder the formation of an authentic, mature self. However, if the decision to cultivate a talent is imposed by the system rather than made by the individual, there is a significant risk that the person will be forced into a life script that fails to address their autonomous needs. This may not only limit development but also amount to a form of coercion.

In the areas described above, well-intentioned efforts by others may result in serious neglect and constraint for 2e individuals. Their emotional needs are especially vulnerable to deprivation. As noted by Wojtyna and Gierczyk (2025), emotional neglect may lead to the emergence of atypical patterns of emotional functioning (see Figure 5.2).

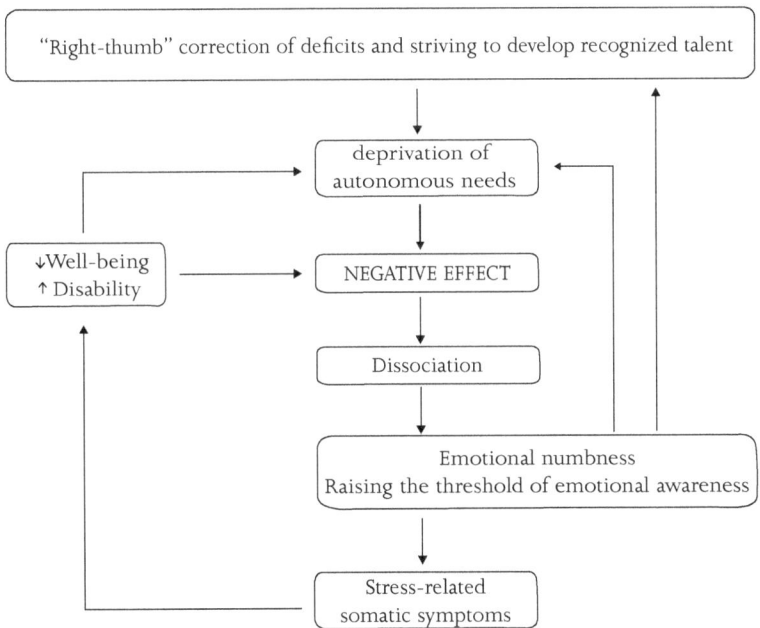

**Figure 5.2** Right-thumb mentality and the emotional functioning of a 2e person

Distress related to the deprivation of emotional needs constitutes a risk factor for the development of a dissociative personality structure. In such cases, the individual detaches from experiences that are unbearable. This phenomenon can lead to a fragmentation of the self into disconnected parts, thereby preventing the formation of an integrated, stable and mature sense of self.

Observations by Wojtyna and Gierczyk (2025) suggest that individuals who experience emotional neglect tend to develop an elevated threshold for emotional awareness. This adaptation facilitates the suppression of unwanted, uncontrollable emotional tension, enabling the individual to continue pursuing their tasks – often related to hypercompensation or the fulfilment of others' needs and ambitions. However, this increased threshold for emotional awareness also impairs the ability to recognize one's own needs and prevents the early detection of internal warning signals.

By the time the individual begins to consciously experience their emotions, it is often too late. The emotional response escalates rapidly, and the capacity for adequate regulation is diminished. This, in turn, adversely affects psychological and relational functioning. There is also a notable risk of intensifying somatic symptoms, which may further impair physical functioning. While the person may not yet be consciously aware of their emotional state, the somatic component of emotional experience emerges immediately. Bodily symptoms are felt but not recognized as emotional in origin. Over time, this can contribute to the development of stress-related somatic disorders and may exacerbate existing disability-related difficulties.

## INCLUSION OR INVALIDATION?

Finally, let us turn our attention to the socio-cultural aspects of inclusivity. The principle of inclusion is founded on the intention to extend respect to all individuals, regardless of the differences we perceive between them. In practice, however, fully realizing this ideal proves difficult.

Modern mentalities tend to demand the formulation of clear and unambiguous behavioural guidelines. In an effort to avoid accusations of discrimination or injustice, there is a growing tendency to create manuals and codes of conduct outlining how to act inclusively. Yet, perceptions of respect – and the specific needs related to it – vary considerably. As a result, there is an increasing push to expand recommendations concerning inclusive behaviours.

At many universities, specialized guidelines have been introduced to guide staff and students in the appropriate language and conduct when interacting with, among others, 2e individuals. Language is a powerful tool through which we express our views on diversity, including disability. It is now widely promoted that we should use the language preferred by a given community or individual and avoid terminology that is harmful, discriminatory or ableist.

At the same time, many researchers show that inclusive language – designed to reduce discrimination, reflect diversity and support social equity – may, in some contexts, paradoxically reinforce perceptions of intergroup difference, depending on the social environment and how the language is employed (Jetten & Spears, 2003; Porter et al., 2016). This introduces a real risk of creating social tensions, both for 2e individuals and for those around them.

A lack of critical reflection on the implementation of inclusive language policies within universities may lead to numerous tensions and unintended conflicts. Let us first consider the perspective of academic staff and non-disabled students. The regulatory imposition of inclusive language may, contrary to the intended spirit of inclusivity, produce the following outcomes:

1. Even in the absence of prejudice toward 2e individuals, the mandatory use of specific language – particularly when a lecturer is unconvinced of its appropriateness – can trigger a negative emotional response. This discomfort may be expressed in subtle ways, such as sarcasm or passive resistance, during interactions with students. Such emotional responses may then be misinterpreted by 2e students as discriminatory or mocking behaviour.
2. The need to concentrate on crafting language that aligns precisely with inclusive standards may compromise clarity of communication or reduce the substantive quality of information conveyed by lecturers. This may, in turn, conflict with the educational needs of the wider student body.
3. There is a significant risk that, even when inclusive language is used consistently and in good faith, one or more students may still feel

offended or invalidated. Sensitivities vary widely, and intent does not always align with perception.
4. Excessive focus on a relatively small group of 2e students may lead to the deprivation of attention to the needs of other students, who constitute the majority. These students may develop a perception that 2e individuals are being unduly favoured. This impression may be further reinforced by awareness of the ongoing public discourse around the potential overdiagnosis within 2e populations. The result may be growing frustration among non-disabled students, a sense of injustice and increased resentment directed toward their 2e peers.

It is also important to consider the issue of inclusive language from the perspective of 2e individuals themselves. Let us take autistic individuals as an example. Within the autistic community, the preferred linguistic convention is often *identity-first language* – referring to oneself as an "autistic person". Nevertheless, many educational and healthcare systems around the world still predominantly use *person-first language* – that is, terms such as "person with autism" or "person with a disability". The intention behind person-first language was to reduce stigma and encourage people not to define others solely by their disability. In many circles, this aim has arguably been achieved. However, a different problem has since emerged.

As previously discussed, autism and disability are not choices; they are formative experiences that reshape a person's entire developmental trajectory. These characteristics influence identity, which is why identity-first language often better reflects the lived reality of 2e individuals. Phrases such as "person with . . ." may misleadingly suggest that autistic or disabled individuals merely *have* these traits, while otherwise developing and functioning in ways similar to the general population. This is a serious distortion, one that risks obscuring the specific developmental needs of 2e individuals and thus failing to meet them.

Of course, every individual may have their own linguistic preferences, and it is important to respect these preferences wherever possible. However, this does not imply a need for rigid adherence to externally imposed forms. What is needed instead is the promotion of self-advocacy – the ability to articulate why a particular linguistic form is meaningful – and the negotiation of communication norms between students, or in student–lecturer relationships.

## RIGHT-THUMB MENTALITY AND 2E INDIVIDUALS – A WAY OUT OF THE DEADLOCK

The reflections presented above lead to the conclusion that contemporary socio-cultural trends – summarized here as the *right-thumb mentality* – pose a significant risk of neglecting the essential needs of 2e individuals, even when actions are motivated by good intentions (see Figure 5.3).

Attempts to codify behavioural rules aimed at reducing the risk of discrimination and harmful treatment may paradoxically lead to increased conflict and a heightened sense of injustice. In response, institutions often feel compelled to expand their codes of conduct and guidance documents by adding new provisions. The number of recommendations grows, yet this does not necessarily translate into meaningful support for the development of students, whether 2e or non-2e.

By contrast, adopting a respect-based perspective invites open engagement between 2e and non-2e individuals, encouraging mutual curiosity, exploration of one another's needs and the discovery of shared and individual strengths. This process of learning through interaction enhances communication skills and deepens cooperation grounded in mutual care. Such an approach supports the development of the authentic self and enables students to make better use of their university experience.

## SUMMARY: BLESSED OR CURSED?

Neglecting emotional needs and failing to support self-agency in 2e individuals increases the risk of identity distortion. Gifted individuals

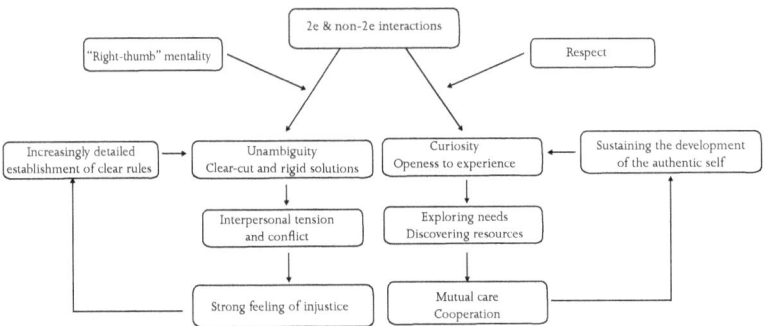

**Figure 5.3** 2e to non-2e interactions based on right-thumb rigid rules vs respect

who are repeatedly misunderstood and deprived of social support may experience feelings of rejection and alienation. They may withdraw, camouflage their true nature or assume a façade to gain social approval. Over time, the authentic self becomes buried beneath layers of adaptation. The pain of feeling "different" can be particularly acute when one's experience is not validated. This can lead to impostor syndrome, self-doubt and persistent anxiety. Meanwhile, individuals with disabilities are often subjected to social marginalization. A lack of recognition of their strengths or value contributes to internalized ableism, a form of self-stigma. Without meaningful opportunities for engagement and development, the identity of these individuals may become reduced to the label of their diagnosis. The coexistence of giftedness and disability in 2e individuals requires nuanced understanding and personalized support.

So what can be done? Firstly, we must adopt a relational perspective: understanding 2e functioning as the outcome of an interaction between the individual and their environment. This shifts the focus from pathology to developmental context. Secondly, we need to cultivate dialogue, not only with the individual and their family, but also across disciplines and institutions. Effective support is rooted in empathy, flexibility and a willingness to see beyond standardized norms. Twice-exceptional individuals can thrive when they are recognized not merely as the sum of their challenges and talents but as whole people whose identities deserve space to develop with dignity. Finally, support must be offered across multiple levels: emotionally (through acceptance and emotional security), socially (through inclusion and authentic belonging) and structurally (through tailored education, healthcare and legal protections). It is only then that 2e individuals can integrate their experiences and grow into their full potential – on their own terms.

**REFERENCES**

Ainsworth, M. D. S., Blehar, M. C., Waters, E. & Wall, S. (2015). *Patterns of attachment: A psychological study of the strange situation.* Lawrence Erlbaum.

Bowlby, J. (1969). *Attachment and loss, Vol. 1: Attachment.* Basic Books.

Frances A. (2013). The new crisis of confidence in psychiatric diagnosis. *Annals of Internal Medicine*, 159(10), 720. https://doi.org/10.7326/0003-4819-159-10-201311190-00021

Hartman, D., O'Donnell-Killen, T., Doyle, J. K., Kavanagh, M., Day, A., & Azevedo, J. (2023). *The adult autism assessment handbook. A neurodiversity-affirmative approach.* Jessica Kingsley Publishers.

Hutchins, H. M. (2015). Outing the imposter: A study exploring imposter phenomenon among higher education faculty. *New Horizons in Adult Education and Human Resource Development*, 27, 3–12. https://doi.org/10.1002/nha3.20098

Hutchins, H. M. & Rainbolt, H. (2017). What triggers imposter phenomenon among academic faculty? A critical incident study exploring antecedents, coping and development opportunities. *Human Resource Development International*, 20, 194–214. https://doi.org/10.1080/13678868.2016.1248205

Jetten, J. & Spears, R. (2003). The divisive potential of differences and similarities: The role of intergroup distinctiveness in intergroup differentiation. *European Review of Social Psychology*, 14(1), 203–241. https://doi.org/10.1080/10463280340000063

Nijenhuis, E. R. S. & van der Hart, O. (2011). Dissociation in trauma: A new definition and comparison with previous formulations. *Journal of Trauma & Dissociation*, 12(4), 416–445. https://doi.org/10.1080/15299732.2011.570592

Okoye, C., Obialo-Ibeawuchi, C. M., Obajeun, O. A., Sarwar, S., Tawfik, C., Waleed, M. S., Wasim, A. U., Mohamoud, I., Afolayan, A. Y. & Mbaezue, R. N. (2023). Early diagnosis of autism spectrum disorder: A review and analysis of the risks and benefits. *Cureus*, 15(8), e43226. https://doi.org/10.7759/cureus.43226

Paris, J. (2015). *Overdiagnosis in psychiatry*. Oxford University Press.

Porter, S. C., Rheinschmidt-Same, M. & Richeson, J. A. (2016). Inferring identity from language: Linguistic intergroup bias informs social categorization. *Psychological Science*, 27(1), 94–102. https://doi.org/10.1177/0956797615612202

Shytle, J. G. (2022). *Twice-exceptional childhood experiences contributing to imposter syndrome in post-secondary faculty*. Walden Dissertation and Doctoral Studies Collection.

Sikora, T. & Górnik-Durose, M. (2013). On the mentality of the contemporary human, its sources and manifestations. In M. Górnik-Durose (Ed.), *Contemporary culture and health* (pp. 15–50). GWP.

Wojtyna, E. & Gierczyk, M. (2025). *Charting the experience of children and adolescents affected by emotional neglect*. Routledge.

Wojtyna, E. & Stawiarska, P. (2013). On the contemporary understanding of health. In M. Górnik-Durose (Ed.), *Contemporary culture and health* (pp. 51–76). GWP.

## Six

*Preparing Students With 2e for Success at University*

Twenty years ago, only those studying children identified as twice-exceptional (2e) or those parenting them had heard of this exceptionality. This minority-of-a-minority of students, researchers and family members represents those at the intersection between gifted students and all students with exceptionalities other than giftedness. Students with 2e[1] may be found in every group of exceptional students except those students with a developmental delay. It's not difficult to conceive of gifted/blind, gifted/deaf, gifted/fragile health or gifted/physical disability, but the others are more difficult to imagine: gifted/learning disabled, gifted/autism spectrum disorder (ASD), gifted/attention deficit hyperactivity disorder (ADHD) or gifted/mental health challenge. It's also common for a student who is 2e to have three or more exceptionalities. It gets complicated.

The field is growing – both in the number of researchers and that of students – and the first group of students with 2e has now reached university. How would you facilitate the learning of Helen Keller or Steven Hawking in your university course? As is typical, teachers in the K–12 system have been aware of and are trying to address the needs of students who have 2e for ten years or more, while the university system lags behind and only now is at the budding awareness stage. This chapter is intended to demystify students with 2e for university faculty members and staff members who work with students with disabilities. It is also intended to provide practical tips for working with them.

According to two Canadian studies, access to post-secondary education for students with disabilities is an equity issue, with ramifications for lifelong earnings (Mohler & Godin-Jacques, 2023) and satisfaction, as well as, one might argue, societal benefits. Yet obstacles to admission to higher education institutions and spotty access to useful accommodations exist. Also, in many cases students must self-advocate

DOI: 10.4324/9781003571674-6

and request access to services and accommodations, placing unfair burdens on students to fight for what rightfully should be provided by institutions (Mohler & Godin-Jacques, 2023; Nelson et al., 2023). Thus, these data "fail to support the notion that education has the potential to be the 'great equalizer' for students with disabilities" (Mohler & Godin-Jacques, 2023, p. 27). We'll begin by discussing what may have led to students with 2e arriving at the university campus.

## IDENTIFICATION ISSUES AS INHIBITORS TO SUCCESS

### Late, Missed or Misidentification as Gifted

Many students with 2e whose giftedness is diagnosed in high school or college experience feelings of failure, worthlessness, low self-esteem, depression, anger or frustration. According to McEachern and Bornot (2001), 41% of gifted students with disabilities in their sample were not diagnosed as gifted until university. These late-diagnosed students with 2e also report negative experiences in school: social isolation (Alamer, 2017); repeated punishment for late work; placement in a self-contained special education class, which may or may not provide instruction tailored for them; grade retention; fraught interactions with certain teachers and peers; difficulty in reading and writing; or low motivation for school (Reis et al., 1997). However, these students credited their outside interests, sports and other activities with enabling them to survive and construct positive attitudes (Reis et al., 1997). Alamer (2017) and Tagtmeyer (2018) conducted case studies of individuals who have 2e, and they claimed that late diagnosis and lack of support at school led to lack of self-understanding and issues with behaviour and mental health. (Note well that while the students may have believed there was a causal relationship, none can be verified by research due to ethical concerns.)

Most often, the aspect of late identification of individuals with 2e by schools is the giftedness, while parents are more likely to recognize the giftedness or both exceptionalities. In their study with gifted/ASD university students, Reis et al. (2022) reported that some of the parents or the students questioned the ASD diagnosis.

Neurological examinations of students with 2e reveal that the two exceptionalities have a lifelong impact on each other (Hua et al., 2014), though one study found that gifted/learning disabled (LD) students think that the exceptionalities are separate (Lummiss, 2018). Another neurological study (Gilger & Olulade, 2013) found when gifted/LD students were considering their strengths, they identified as gifted, while when considering their challenges, they thought of themselves as LD. Gilger and Olulade (2013) also reported that a reading disability interacts with giftedness throughout the life of a person with 2e; compensations for the disability change the way their brain as an adult processes text and spatial data.

Late identification of giftedness plays a role in the identity formation of students who have 2e. They (and their parents) sometimes find it hard to believe that they could be both gifted and disabled (Reis et al., 1997; Reis et al., 2022). Their identification with a disability may have led to negative perceptions by teachers and sometimes parents (Reis et al., 1997). There were instances of students who did not receive support for either or both of their exceptionalities, and their subsequent achievement was depressed (Reis et al., 1997). There is evidence that a learning disability in particular can have serious, negative effects on a person's lifelong potential to fulfil their cognitive strengths or gifts because of experiences such as lack of practice, emphasis on reading improvement (mostly focused on decoding) and overuse of the brain's right hemisphere to compensate for left hemisphere inadequacies (Gilger & Olulade, 2013).

There are especially negative influences on identity formation for Black males: they are identified as gifted at less than half the rate of white males. Black males are more often identified with only a disability, thereby excluding them from rigorous courses and experiences (Harris et al., 2016; Mayes et al., 2019). Consequently, they are less prepared for university and careers and more likely to experience negative interactions with teachers and peers (Mayes et al., 2019).

## WAYS FOR HIGH SCHOOLS TO HELP PREPARE STUDENTS WITH 2E

Accessing AP, IB, Honours or Other Challenging Academic Experiences
As Tagtmeyer (2018) suggests, university should not be the first place where a student is intellectually challenged. However, students who have 2e whose giftedness is not recognized often find themselves in very restrictive settings, thus limiting their university and career readiness. This is particularly true for some marginalized groups, including

Black males (Harris et al., 2016; Mayes et al., 2019). In fact, some school districts have practices whereby students with a disability are not allowed to take AP, IB, honours, concurrent enrolment in high school and university, or other types of challenging courses (hereafter, "challenging courses"); only allowing opportunities to take such courses to those students who are highly academically successful; or designating one teacher (typically the instructor of the challenging course) to determine who may take the course. Needless to say, students with exceptional needs are generally excluded (Schultz, 2012). Another limitation that bars students with 2e from challenging courses is that guidance counsellors or parents may advise students with disabilities to enrol in classes that are not consistent with the student's post-secondary goals and aspirations, and/or discourage their interest in careers requiring university credentials (Schultz, 2012).

In a qualitative interview study (Reis et al., 2022), several participants with 2e on the autism spectrum discussed the need for more engagement and challenge in their high school classes. Others recommended providing high school students with varied learning opportunities that address more in-depth thinking, creativity, critical thinking and study skills, and stated that those experiences built in them more perseverance and confidence.

Thus, completing appropriately rigorous courses greatly assists in preparing students for the academic challenges of university (Reis et al., 2022, 2023). Some students credit the challenging classes they completed in areas of interest during high school as one of the most important reasons that they succeeded academically (Reis et al., 2023). The successful completion of at least one challenging course and/or a project that they chose gave them a realistic glimpse of the type of work they would encounter in university. A particularly beneficial method of advanced study for that purpose is dual or concurrent enrolment, where a school district develops a partnership with a university (either in person or online). The students who are gifted and those with 2e take a university course in their area of interest and receive both high school and university credit (Reis et al., 2023).

An adult mentor, such as a teacher in special education or regular education, a guidance counsellor or a parent, was often involved and, in some cases instigated, the enrolment of a student with 2e in challenging classes. In one-on-one discussion with the student, they served as cheerleaders, calling out the student's strengths, pointing to aspects of the student's excellent work related to the specific course they are contemplating, and provided the encouragement to at least sign up and try it (Schultz, 2012).

### Out-of-School Experiences

Multiple studies (e.g. Harris et al., 2016; Madaus et al., 2023; Mayes et al., 2019; Reis et al., 2022) have noted that a high number of students with 2e took part in sports, clubs and other extracurricular activities. Most students experimented with multiple activities, persevering and honing the mix until "finding the right fit for their talents and interests" (Reis et al., 2023, p. 385). Not only does such participation develop their expertise in the chosen field, but it also helps the students in other ways: developing social networks, increasing social understanding (Madaus et al., 2023; Tagtmeyer, 2018) and developing ability to work together on a common goal. In an area in which the student demonstrates skill of a high order, they might assume leadership roles with peers (Reis et al., 2022). Balancing extracurriculars with challenging courses and home responsibilities also helps students to learn how to manage their time (Reis et al., 2023).

Another valuable experience during the high school years is participation in residential gifted programmes. These programmes help them learn to live independently, socialize with others, communicate more clearly, practise time management and organizational skills, and acclimate to a university campus (Reis et al., 2022, 2023).

These types of positive outof-school experiences enabled students with 2e to survive and constructively perceive their negative school experiences, leading to positive attitudes and setting them up for later success (Reis et al., 1997).

### Understanding Their Own Strengths and Needs

Another benefit of both out-of-school experiences and challenging courses, normally undertaken in areas of high interest, is a better understanding of one's academic strengths and needs. The same seems to be true of completing independent and small group projects. Given that these experiences are intended to stretch the student's capabilities, students encounter difficulties and need to develop strategies to address them or request that an accommodation be considered.

Teachers play two important roles with respect to students' understanding of their strengths and needs: they recognize and specifically identify where students' academic talents lie, and they provide encouragement and give them confidence to take academic risks (Reis et al., 2022, 2023). Successfully completing challenging courses or independent studies helps them to develop additional confidence.

Having students sit in on and eventually lead their own individualized education programme (IEP) meetings in high school (where their strengths, needs and the instructional strategies to address both are set out for the year) is an effective way to help them better comprehend their academic profile. It is important for the student to be knowledgeable about their profile. In a study of gifted/ASD students, Reis and colleagues (2022) found that those students who did not understand their ASD in high school continued to struggle with knowing their strengths and weaknesses in their higher education settings. This confusion can contribute to poor choices of elective courses, topics for projects, future aspirations and programmes of study appropriate to their strengths (Reis et al., 1997).

### Choosing a Major Aligned With Strengths

Understanding one's academic profile is important when choosing a programme of study or major. Considerations include choosing a direction:

- where they have strengths and interests;
- which does not rely on mastering many new compensation strategies;
- which does not require proficiency in bodies of knowledge or skills that are negatively impacted by their disability; or
- where the disability negatively impacts their performance (Reis et al., 1997).

In cases where students do not develop sufficient or necessary compensation strategies during their high school years or earlier, but are able to take advantage of workshops and/or tutoring for this purpose at university, it should be possible for them to choose courses and/or majors in which their talents can flourish (Reis et al., 2000). Choosing a major that is well aligned with one's strengths is key because there is some evidence suggesting that students who select a major in line with their strengths are more likely to graduate (Snyder et al., 2022).

### Developing Support Networks

Parents are the first and most enduring advocates. Normally they play significant roles in having both their child's talents and challenges recognized and supported. To maximize the student's talents, they deter the schools from taking the easy route of focusing solely on the disability and advocate strongly for the giftedness to be developed. They fight for the necessary accommodations. These parents expect their children to attend university, and they expect the school to academically prepare them for that (Schultz, 2012).

Parental support, of course, continues into university and beyond. They help students get along with others, provide financial support, learn how to manage their medications and provide driving lessons – or if not, teach their children to read bus, subway or train schedules and find the right embarking point. They visit university campuses with their child and help them with their final choice. They listen and give emotional support (Armstrong, 2018; Reis et al., 1997).

Students build social networks as they go through school. While some friends come and go quickly, others are more steadfast. Students who have 2e can add and delete friends from social media as everyone else does. As they enter university, these social networks provide emotional support as well as answers to questions from a known ally. Even a pet can "visit" on a live chat (Reis et al., 2023).

Not to be underestimated are the roles of teachers and guidance counsellors. Teachers can provide support to take academic risks, bolster the students' confidence, and acknowledge their gifts. Some teachers advocate with other teachers for the right of a student with 2e to accommodations, and as the student gets close to graduation, take them along to model this skill. They can talk to the students about their university experiences, while guidance counsellors may have knowledge of which universities have strong programmes in the student's area(s) of interest. Those teachers who were most helpful to the student will likely allow them to maintain contact once they are at university and continue to provide support. Later, certain professors may assume the roles of instructor, role model, mentor and advisor for all types of issues.

Teachers and other school personnel can provide information to students about ways that university is different from high school. These include new locations and casts of characters; more independence for coursework, time management and organization; changes in how courses are structured, managed and scheduled; rules for, access to and types of accommodations; and the out-of-class social experiences (Trevisan et al., 2021). Regarding accommodations, the students should be aware that there will be fewer accommodations available to them at university, and they normally will need outside testing to access them; there will be fewer types of accommodations; and they normally will need to take a role in making faculty aware of them and in receiving them.

At the end of their high school experience, as students and families start to explore specific colleges, secondary teams can provide useful information about the range of services and supports that are available. For example, students and families can be informed that some campuses have specific programmes for students with 2e and ASD while others offer more generic disability support services (Madaus et al., 2023).

## CHALLENGES IN TRANSITIONING TO UNIVERSITY

The US-based National Technical Assistance Center on Transition (NTACT) of the US Department of Education (n.d.) focuses specifically on transition of students with disabilities to college or the workplace, and provides a wealth of resources and information. Their online chart on predictors of post-school success is particularly helpful.

Gifted Black male students with disabilities may need advocacy skills to access accommodations for university admission tests (if any). They may also need to be made aware that universities normally have cultural centres, offices for students with disabilities and academic support, and where they may find these places (Mayes et al., 2019).

### Independent Living Skills

For most students, these are absorbed through observation and helping with chores at their parents' home, but some students with 2e may need specific instruction in a range of skills:

- setting and maintaining a schedule (including time for study, cleaning, grocery shopping, laundry, etc.);
- personal hygiene;

- transportation (Madaus et al., 2023);
- personal safety (including crisis management) (Tagtmeyer, 2018);
- managing medications (Madaus et al., 2023; Tagtmeyer 2018); and
- sleep and relaxation.

Social Skills

Students who have 2e may at first feel lonely and isolated in a new environment (Armstrong, 2018). A lack of friends may stem from not knowing how to initiate conversations with new contacts (Armstrong, 2018; Madaus et al., 2022; Tagtmeyer, 2018). There may be workshops on developing social and/or communication skills at the university, or the student's roommate or another ally may role-play with them and explain what they are missing and how to correct it. Another excellent arena for learning and practising these skills is in student clubs and activities in the student's area of interest (Madaus et al., 2022; Reis et al., 2023). They will be comfortable with the content and able to focus on interaction. Clubs and activities are logical places to make friends and also address anxiety while building connections (Armstrong, 2018).

More nuanced social skills would involve learning about social dynamics and perspective, understanding others' perceptions of oneself (Armstrong, 2018; Tagtmeyer, 2018), developing pro-social behaviour (Armstrong, 2018) and improving their interpretation of social cues (Reis et al., 2023). Perhaps viewing a movie, reality show or soap opera with a friend who can point out examples of the targeted skill or behaviour would be helpful.

Communication Skills

Communication skills often accompany social skills and the two may be difficult to separate. Direct, concrete examples and role play may assist in clearly sending and correctly interpreting verbal and non-verbal messages (Tagtmeyer, 2018), completing group projects or listening to others and then figuring out how to interact without talking over others (Madaus et al., 2023). Clubs and activities may assist in communicating clearly and explaining facts, skills or procedures to others (Reis et al., 2023).

It is important for a student with 2e to be able to understand that one speaks differently (verbally or electronically) with a parent, professor, romantic interest, casual friend (Madaus et al., 2023) and lab partner. Having someone role-play these situations and then generating one's own examples should be helpful.

There are two tricky situations where students may flounder without specific guidance. When adjusting to different living situations, which often occurs repeatedly throughout university, it is important to reflect on the skill of understanding other perspectives. Using specific phrases, such as "the way that this works for me is . . . how does it work best for you?", emphasizes to the student that not everything will be completely congruent with their preferences. They need to decide which are the most important considerations and focus on satisfactory conclusions for those few.

The second tricky situation is communicating with professors. The student with 2e may be reluctant to approach the professor. Some universities leave the onus for communicating accommodations to the student. The idea of "accommodating" a student implies that the professor is the one who decides if an accommodation will be allowed. Hua et al. (2014) recommend thinking of the interaction as a "negotiation" between the student and the professor (as two adults) where they would be on a *somewhat* more equal footing.

For all private conversations with professors, there may be different rules for contact, e.g. speaking after class, before class, only by email, only during office hours, etc. If the professor does not explain their preference on the first day of class, the student should ask them after class how they should make arrangements to talk privately (Madaus et al., 2023).

### Mental Health, Emotional Management and Coping Skills

Nearly all universities have counselling or emotional support offices, which should be clearly communicated to all students at the beginning of each semester. These offices deal with a wide range of issues and know whom to contact for more specialized support if needed. Many types of emotional concerns (e.g. stress, anxiety, depression, isolation, loneliness, fatigue) can make a student reluctant to seek help. Other impediments to seeking counselling services may include fear of being bullied or othered or a desire to "prove oneself" (Armstrong, 2018; Madaus et al., 2023).

Some students find that counselling helps in addressing negative messages from past educational experiences (Reis et al., 2000). Other situations facilitated by counselling include constructive ways to handle emotions (Tagtmeyer, 2018) and resolving impacts of intersectional identities (such as LGTBQ+, race, gender) (Tagtmeyer, 2018).

In addition to individual counselling, the university may be running support groups for students who are dealing with similar issues. Students may find that meeting others who struggle as they do to be reassuring. Connections with their support systems (on campus or online) can also be very important (Reis et al., 2022).

### Fear of Self-Disclosing the Disability

Nearly 75% of students with disabilities do not disclose them (Madaus et al., 2024). Some reasons for this may be fear of stigmatization, bullying or being "othered"; or a campus climate that is unaccepting of differences (Killean & Hubka, 1999; Nelson et al., 2023). In most cases (including informing a professor of the need for accommodations), the student may find that if they talk about some of their challenges in specific terms, they may not need to disclose the specific disability.

### Faculty Teaching Styles

Of course, students can do little about this. Faculty members usually teach in ways that are comfortable and familiar to themselves, which don't necessarily benefit the students' learning (Armstrong, 2018). With some very approachable professors, a student might ask the professor to share their notes or presentation, etc. The best source of information about professors, or even ones to take for certain courses is other students. By the end of the first semester, students with 2e should know some other students with disabilities and be able to find professors from whom other students successfully learned for a given course (Armstrong, 2018; Reis et al., 2000). This can be easily accomplished if the university has a social or interest-based club or team for students with disabilities.

## SUGGESTED SERVICES TO BE PROVIDED BY UNIVERSITIES

Ames et al. (2022) provided extensive evidence of the scarcity of supports for students with ASD at Canadian universities. Of 258 publicly funded institutions researched, only 15 offered any type of supports, with an average of 2.4 types, the most common of which was including some information on the institution's website. One would speculate that more supports would be needed by students with ASD than with other disabilities due to the complexity of the exceptionality. However, experience indicates that very few institutions provide more than minimal supports such as accommodations for note-taking and test-taking, which often are available to all students. In an online survey, eighteen of the 36 universities indicated autism-specific supports, with the most represented being transition-to-university services (generic to all students), social groups and peer mentoring. Supports were acknowledged to facilitate independence, a sense of community and legitimization of neurodivergent experiences (Coombs et al., 2023). This highlights the finding that the available academic supports and accommodations often fail to address the scope of needs and abilities of students with autism, not to mention all of the other exceptionalities (Canadian Academy of Health Sciences, 2022).

A similar study in the US (Nachman et al., 2022) found 74 programmes to support ASD students, mostly in four-year public institutions in the mid-Atlantic region. This represents 2.2% of public not-for-profit institutions in the US, a percentage which had more than doubled the amount between 2012 and 2017. Unfortunately, this leaves huge areas of the country where services are unavailable.

What follows is a chronological compilation of an ideal set of support services for students who have 2e and are going to university, beginning at the time of the student's initial search for the university they will attend.

### Information About Services

Universities need to inform all prospective students in multiple ways about the services they offer for students with disabilities: course calendars/catalogues, acceptance packages, websites, in-person information sessions, posters on campus, etc. The information needs to include the services and supports available to students with disabilities, and whether they are tailored for students with disabilities or available to all students, the eligibility criteria for each, and whom to contact and where to go for additional details (Killean & Hubka, 1999).

### Orientation Programme

Many universities hold orientation sessions for all incoming students, but having an orientation especially designed for students with 2e (or even for all students with disabilities) is a more effective strategy. The main purposes would be to reduce anxiety, help the students with 2e learn to navigate available resources, introduce a dedicated resource person and allow students to meet their peers. A campus tour might include some resources expressly designed for students with 2e and describe how to access them (e.g. disability office, adaptive technology lab, low stimulus spaces). Other resources to point out, such as tutoring centres and career services, would be for all students. Additional optional activities may have no permanent meeting place but should be discussed, such as social groups and peer-advocacy groups (Madaus et al., 2023). There should also be specific information regarding safety, emergency and evacuation procedures (Killean & Hubka, 1999). Another topic to include is how accommodations differ in university as opposed to high school, and that they might need an assessment prior to accessing accommodations. If possible, this information should be included prominently in all students' acceptance package, with contact information for those to whom it applies.

### Dedicated Contact Person

Someone on campus should have part or all of their responsibilities set aside for working with students who have 2e, and they should meet with these students early in the term, ideally at orientation (Madaus et al., 2023). Depending on the number of students with 2e in a given year, this person may be supported by graduate or undergraduate peer mentors. The contact person should serve as a clearinghouse where students go to address given needs, and assist students early with advice regarding courseload, roommate situations, etc. As time goes on, students with 2e may confer with the contact person for ongoing advice and troubleshooting. The students should be strongly encouraged to contact the dedicated resource when things start to become uncomfortable, before their GPA (grade point average) is affected. Here, "uncomfortable" is not synonymous with "difficult", because university work should be challenging; rather it means that they feel lost, they can see that they are falling behind, someone is bullying them, etc. (Armstrong, 2018; Madaus et al., 2023).

All students, especially students with 2e, should be able to ask for help and know when and how to access help. As they become more familiar with the campus and the support provided by various offices, students' need for the dedicated contact person will likely decrease.

### Advice on Courseload

Reis et al. (2000) recommend that students who have 2e consider a reduced courseload, at least for the first year, in order to learn how much extra time they might need to balance the number of courses with their own learning profile. Once they feel comfortable with the balance, they might feel as if they can handle a full courseload; if not, however, the student may need to request a change in the time limits, if any, to programme completion (Killean & Hubka 1999).

### Accommodations

The time is long past when accommodation referred only to physical accessibility to the campus, each building and washrooms (bathrooms/ toilets). The types of accommodations for students with 2e, except for those with physical or mobility exceptionalities, are likely to be invisible and more nuanced. In any case, academic staff should be notified early that an incoming student requires accommodations (Armstrong, 2018), and the student may be encouraged to speak to the programme chair as well. Early notification may help to acquire texts and/or research materials in an alternative format (Killean & Hubka, 1999), for example, so speaking with the programme chair may facilitate that. This will assist the student in completing work in a timely manner.

The most commonly requested accommodations are provision of a note-taker and extra time for exams. It should not be the student's responsibility to acquire a note-taker, as this sometimes results in poor service, frustration (Killean & Hubka, 1999) or unwanted disclosure of disabilities. The preferred alternative is for accommodations to be centrally administered, commonly through the disability office. Regarding exams, extra time and/or a private space generally also are administered through a disability office, particularly for final exams where space is at a premium. If the student requires an exam in an alternate format, this should be provided for them free of charge (Killean & Hubka, 1999).

In addition to note-takers and exam accommodations, students with 2e may need some other, more specialized, accommodations, such as texts in alternative media, specialized technology or permission to leave the room briefly to reduce stress. Some of these may be facilitated by the disabilities office, while others will need to be negotiated with each instructor.

*Adaptive Technology*

Thought should be given to the location of adaptive technology and software. It is preferable for them to be centralized near, within or linked to other facilities such as a library or alternative format services. Unless a student is already familiar with the use of the technology/software, training should be provided. If a student has successfully used a software program previously, the university should consider purchasing it, finding a grant to assist, etc. It is also important for adaptive technology to be located within at least some of the computer labs open to all students. If new technology is to be acquired, students who will be using that equipment should be consulted (Killean & Hubka, 1999).

*Social Activities/Interest-Based Clubs*

As noted earlier, these types of activities can be extremely helpful for students with 2e in several ways: building social and communication skills, peer relationships, informal information about courses, accommodations and so on. They can be important in combating loneliness, depression or anxiety. Depending on the number of students with disabilities at the university, there may be a need for groups targeted specifically for students who have 2e (Armstrong, 2018; Madaus et al., 2023). In some cases, it may even be advantageous to provide clubs specifically for given types of 2e (i.e. gifted/learning disabled, gifted/ASD, gifted/ADHD, etc.).

*Lower-Stimulus Spaces*

This type of space is particularly necessary for gifted/ASD students, but may be helpful for others who experience sensory overload or overstimulation (Madaus et al., 2023; Tagtmeyer, 2018). A safe space to move away from noises, crowds or fraught interactions (Reis et al., 2023) may be necessary for some students to survive and succeed at university.

*Mentoring and Tutoring (Peer or Adult)*

Mentoring refers to a longer-term, intensive, almost apprentice-type relationship, while tutoring has a more limited scope, perhaps a single term or course. Shared interests or experiences can form the basis for pairing mentees and mentors (Armstrong, 2018, Nelson et al., 2023). The interpersonal relationship may meet socio-emotional needs as well as academic ones. The mentor may also help the student to navigate services that may be disconnected (Nelson et al., 2023). Training for mentors is recommended, as is regular meetings with mentees.

Simon Fraser University in British Columbia, Canada, operates a peer-mentoring programme called the Autism Mentorship Initiative (AMI), which could be an exemplar for such programmes. Most of the practices of the programme could benefit students with 2e and other exceptionalities. To begin, they interview both mentees and mentors and use those data to match the mentors with mentees. There is an orientation for new mentors to provide individualized support for their mentees, but AMI is not intended to help with assignments, nor are the mentors counsellors. The mentees are expected to formulate goals relating to their personal, academic, social and/or professional lives, along with action plans for achieving them. Both mentees and mentors sign up for the entire academic year, and many sign up more than once. AMI also provides social events and seminars. Research on AMI found that the programme promotes adjustment to university and benefits both mentee and mentor, but does not improve academic performance (Trevisan et al., 2021). Other excellent mentoring programmes are offered at York University (Toronto, Ontario, Canada, 2024), the University of Calgary (Calgary, Alberta, Canada) and Universite Laval (Quebec City, Quebec, Canada; Aschaiek, 2024).

Tutoring programmes are intended for course-specific or assignment-specific assistance. Effective programmes align meticulously with the course or programme curriculum, commit to developing relationships between tutors and students, provide support and training for tutors, and conduct regular formative assessments of students (Michael, 2016).

### Funding

There may be funding from the government, private agencies or advocacy groups, or the institution itself (Ames, 2022). Funds may be needed for purchasing expensive technology or software or to access testing services (Killean & Hubka, 1999). Access to testing is important because services may be predicated on an assessment that supports the students' claim that they have a disability. Testing can be expensive, and a high number of students may need testing "on entry" for "annually". There are several options for institutions, rather than placing this burden on students: provide testing free or for a nominal sum on campus, share the expense for private testing with another nearby post-secondary institution, seek support from government agencies by making them aware of the problems students are facing, or lobby the healthcare organization for the area (Killean & Hubka, 1999).

### Disability-Specific Supports

Just as compensation strategies and accommodations must be individualized to address the specific needs of each student, so must disability offices consider the needs for supports across and within disability groups. Compensations or accommodations common to many students within disability groups will be described later.

Because of the complexity of the exceptionality, there are a number of support areas necessary for gifted students with ASD to thrive at university. These include transition services, residence life planning, peer mentoring and support groups, tutoring, academic accommodations and counselling, life skills coaching, access to internships, cooperative education and specialized campus employment services (Canadian Academy of Health Sciences, 2022, p 19).

## STRATEGIES FOR SUCCESS

In this section, two strategies that are commonly needed and that have been found to be very effective for all or most students with 2e will be discussed, followed by specific compensation strategies.

### Self-Advocacy

In order to request accommodations or ask for help with a new concept from a professor, adjust to a roommate or work effectively with peers on a project, a student with 2e must develop and use advocacy skills. This requires that students know and can clearly explain to others their areas of strength and weakness (Reis et al., 2000). Students with 2e will enter university with varying levels of advocacy skills. Some universities provide a workshop (often during orientation) and have established peer-to-peer groups on self-advocacy where students can strengthen and practise their skills. When students can advocate for themselves, they build their confidence, independence and self-determination (Alamer, 2017; Armstrong, 2018; Madaus et al., 2023).

Effective self-advocacy implies respect for the other party, and it should never be used to avoid work. The key is to find an alternative of equal difficulty and workload to draw upon the student's strengths, taking into consideration the skill/s that are challenging. With faculty members, it is a good idea for the student to have in mind a suggestion that is on topic, equally difficult as the regular assignment and feasible for the student with 2e. In a peer group, early in the process, the student who has 2e should suggest examples of work that they can achieve, rather than wait and be delegated something unworkable for them.

### Independent Projects/Internships

Inquiry- or strengths-based learning in the form of supervised, independent, undergraduate research has been associated with gains in writing, communication and personal skills, and academic functioning (Hu et al., 2008; Hua et al., 2014). This type of project is a good example of something the student might suggest to a professor to replace another kind of assignment. With a little creativity, links can be found between a student's area(s) of interest and the curriculum of most courses. Carefully designed independent studies can strengthen students' critical thinking, problem-solving, reflective judgement, intrinsic motivation and enthusiasm. Projects ideally would develop students' capacity to consider complex ideas and the ways that ideas are connected (Hu et al., 2008; Lee & Ritchotte, 2018; Willard-Holt et al., 2013) An example could be a city thinking of tearing down an old and dilapidated area and replacing it with low-cost housing. This could be studied through a political, economic, ecological, sociological or historical lens, three of which students choose. This type of project may help to clarify, focus or, alternatively, expand an area of interest. Students may find ways in which they can contribute to the community and be a successful adult (Tagtmeyer, 2018).

Small group projects are similarly beneficial, given that the student with 2e shares an area of interest/expertise with their work partners and the capability to work with other students. The same benefits accrue, in addition to learning how to collaborate, which is critical in most workplaces (Tagtmeyer, 2018).

In interviews, some students who have 2e cited independent projects and the freedom to choose their own projects as their favourite part of university. Projects help with other skills and traits, such as managing time, meeting deadlines, filtering distractions and persevering to complete the work. The one downside to independent projects is that a student may become so involved with their project that they ignore their other coursework. This is something particularly common for 2e students with ASD (Reis et al., 2023). Establishing checkpoints along the way with deadlines attached should help to address this potential problem.

### Compensatory Strategies

Students will already know some compensations that work for them, but may need to find additional ones to address more difficult and/or complex work. Whether they learn them in middle school, high school or university, using compensation strategies is the single most common suggestion for students who have 2e (Lee & Ritchotte, 2018; Reis et al., 1997, 2000, 2022, 2023; Willard-Holt et al., 2013). Postsecondary students with disabilities who used learning strategies (a subset of compensatory strategies) were 2.4 times more likely to graduate (O'Neill et al., 2012).

Reis et al. (1997, 2000) delineated various types of compensation strategies, and most of the strategies in this section are paraphrased or expanded from those authors. Strategies coming from a different source are labelled as such. The first subcategory of compensation strategies is called *cognitive/learning* strategies. Included here are memory strategies such as mnemonics, repetition or imagery; rehearsal using flash cards; chunking information into smaller units; identifying key points; and having another person orally explain difficult concepts. Reading strategies form a subcategory. Faggella-Luby et al. (2019) found that many compensation strategies to improve reading focused on word-level decoding rather than on fluency or reading comprehension, where students with 2e should be working.

Reis et al. (1997, 2000) derived the following *study and performance* strategies working with gifted/LD students, but they probably generalize to other students with 2e: note-taking (or having notes taken by another student or by using technology); test-taking preparation; library skills; written expression; reading fluency and comprehension (e.g. SQ3R – survey, question, read, recite and review); and mathematical processing. Developing an independent project would also draw on many of these skills, in addition to critical (and perhaps creative depending on the product) thinking.

Many of the *technological support* tools we take for granted in 2025 were not widely used in 1997 or 2000, but an exhaustive search revealed no other strategies that have been studied with students who have 2e. This category includes word processing; use of computers; recorded books; and textbooks and library resources in alternative formats.

By far the largest category is *executive functions*. Behaviours associated with executive functions are self-talk; organization and time management; dividing assignments into manageable parts over time; prioritizing tasks and goals; filtering distractions and avoiding interesting but irrelevant paths; and initiating work rather than procrastinating. *Metacognition* is similar to executive functions. Metacognition is related to thinking about one's thinking; and impulse control, attention, working memory and cognitive flexibility. The work of Baum and Olenchak (2002), Hua et al. (2014), Lee and Ritchotte (2018) Madaus et al. (2023), Reis et al. (2022), Tagtmeyer (2018) and Willard-Holt et al. (2013) is gratefully acknowledged for their contributions to this section.

### WORKSHOPS TO DEVELOP SKILLS

Both students and faculty members would benefit from workshops to learn the skills to deal with the other group! Students may need to learn a skill over several sessions and attend multiple different workshops. For most faculty members and staff, one workshop lasting one to two hours is likely sufficient, but they may need a refresher after a few years to learn new strategies, or go into greater depth on specific exceptionalities. For motivated faculty members and staff in direct contact with learners who have 2e, several workshops building on the first should be available. Some universities provide certificates recognizing advanced training for employees and/or students on specified topics, and/or students may add workshops they attend to their activity log.

### Workshops for Students

Several mandatory workshops may be offered for students with 2e, ideally during orientation.

#### Mandatory Workshops for All Students With 2e

These should occur as early as possible during the academic year.

*Safety*: what the emergency signals sound like, what to do in a fire drill or other emergency (particularly for students who use wheelchairs or other mobility aids); being safe on campus at night; what to do outside on campus in an emergency, etc.

*Work habits*: developing a weekly schedule and sticking to it; avoiding distractions; monitoring daily, weekly and monthly assignments and activities; dividing assignments into manageable parts over time; avoiding procrastinating. These and other behaviours are also attributed to executive functioning compensations.

*Self-advocacy* (Reis et al., 2000): this is often the most terror-evoking prospect of going to university for students with 2e. This could be two sessions or more, providing time for students to practise (with peers or a staff member). Sharing student experiences with the intervening practice and doing additional peer work might comprise a second session.

*Library skills* (Reis et al., 2000): usually taught by a librarian, sometimes with a professor. Specific library skills for students who have 2e – where the library is; detailed tour of the library showing what is available (e.g. individual study carrels, pods, maker spaces, specialized technology); behaviours to strive for and avoid; using group study rooms; accessing reserve materials, books, etc.

#### Optional Workshops

Optional workshops may be targeted to a specific group, or be more general.

A workshop focused on *study strategies* would incorporate such topics as note-taking, how to study, test-taking preparation, mnemonics, repetition or imagery; rehearsal using flash cards; chunking information into smaller units; and identifying key points (Reis et al., 2000).

Students might need to focus on sustaining *motivation*. Motivating self-talk could include the career they aspire to and what a difference they would make. Students with 2e should be aware that successful university graduates dedicate maximum effort and long hours of hard work (Reis et al., 2000). Podcasts or a presentation by upper-year students with 2e could also be helpful.

Students needing course-related performance strategies (reading comprehension, written expression and mathematical processing) could access the university's reading and writing centre, maths lab and/or tutors. For students with disabilities, it is most helpful if the instructor models the correct structure/procedure first and then facilitates the students' practice (McGuire et. al, 1991; Reis et al., 2000).

### Workshops for Faculty and Student Affairs Staff

These workshops might be presented by a senior student affairs staff member who has successfully guided students with disabilities to succeed and/or by a faculty member who specializes in education for students with disabilities. "Students with disabilities" is used here because many people are not familiar with the term "students who are twice-exceptional".

A clarification: those students with disabilities who aspired to attend university, met the admission criteria, have a support system and survived high school are likely twice-exceptional, even if their giftedness has never been identified. The number of students identifying as 2e in universities is increasing. Thus, it behooves faculty members and student affairs staff to educate themselves about this group of students.

One important topic that should come early in the workshops is faculty instructional styles that are facilitative or inhibitory to the success of students with 2e. Madaus et al. (2023) listed a set of these practices, specifically in a study with 2e students with ASD, but they likely apply to most students with 2e (see Box).

> **Faculty Instruction**
>
> Facilitative practices:
>
> - provide clarity in their course requirements and instruction;
> - allow more freedom and flexibility with deadlines;
> - break things down in a way that all can understand;
> - provide notes in advance; and
> - use several different elements within course sessions (PowerPoint slides, real-life examples, etc.).
>
> Inhibitory practices:
>
> - provide no notes and/or online materials;
> - lecture only without supporting visual materials;
> - fail to translate knowledge to students' level;
> - teach in a disorganized or unclear manner; and
> - proceed too quickly.

Another study (Willard-Holt et al., 2013) with students with 2e, ranging from grade 8 to post-graduates, found providing *choice* as the main factor in all of these students' success. Having *control of their own learning*, such as in independent study, and *working with complex ideas and ways of thinking*, were very beneficial strategies.

Most of these topics for workshops are applicable to student affairs/office for disability support staff as well as faculty members (Baum et al., 2014; Lee & Ritchotte, 2018; Mann, 2006; Rubenstein et al., 2015; Willard-Holt et al., 2013). The topics could be combined or split depending on local needs.

- Creating a psychologically safe campus environment; fostering positive relationships
- Asynchronous development and its impact in the classroom
- "Invisible disabilities" (Killean & Hubka, 1999)
- Characteristics of individual exceptionalities (currently the most prevalent: ADHD, ASD, learning disabilities and giftedness)
- Types of accommodations beyond note-takers and extra time for tests, and how they fit with individual disabilities

- Academic and social experiences and needs of incoming students with 2e, presented by current students who have 2e (Reis et al., 2023, specifically regarding gifted students with autism)

Disability awareness training sessions might form part of the agenda for departmental meetings across campus (Killean & Hubka, 1999). The following topics are applicable to interested faculty members.

- Facilitative and inhibitory classroom practices (see the "Faculty Instruction" box)
- Establishing and explaining assignment criteria and sharing exemplars from former students (Lee & Ritchotte, 2018; Willard-Holt et al., 2013)
- Techniques for delivering content fairly for all students (Mohler & Godin-Jacques, 2023)
- Fair and meaningful accommodations
- Deliberately teaching study/learning and performance strategies as applicable to their department or course (Lee & Ritchotte, 2018; Reis et al., 2000; Willard-Holt et al., 2013)
- Providing alternate assignments of equal difficulty
- Encouraging students to pursue topics of interest at their own pace

**CONCLUSION**

Our instinct is to think of people with 2e as exceedingly rare – such as one in a million –but the true figure is much higher. The number of undergraduate students with disabilities in the US and in Canada has approximately doubled in the last 7–10 years, and is now nearly 20% in both countries (National Center for Education Statistics, 2023; Canadian Survey on Disability, 2017 to 2022, 2023). In the US, 66% of high school graduates go on to university; in Canada the figure is 73%. In the US K–12 system the percentage of students with 2e is about 10% (Foley-Nicpon & Teriba, 2022; Nelson et al., 2023). That means 1–2% of the first-year intake might be 2e. Doing all one can to retain these students is good for the university and the students. In addition, some of the chapter's recommendations might also benefit students who have no recognized disabilities.

Research interest on students with 2e is exploding internationally; publication statistics in the field demonstrate increases in articles relating to university students with disabilities of 1,400% from 2013 to 2022 (Madaus et al., 2024). Recent trends in international practices include enrolling students with cognitive disabilities in the higher education international arena (Rillotta & O'Donovan, 2023), structured mentorship of students with disabilities at the graduate level (Sukhai & Latour, 2023) and recognizing "accessibility" as a legitimate field of study (Madaus et al., 2024). Each of these tendencies is congruent with the chapter's recommendations.

It has been anecdotally noted that students with 2e often demonstrate innovative ideas and solutions to problems. They may be able to help us solve tomorrow's knotty problems, but they need the academic preparation of higher education. Higher education teachers and professors are in a unique situation to help students with 2e shine. The world could use more great problem-solvers.

**NOTE**

1 Using person-first phraseology, "2e" in "students with 2e" or "persons who have 2e" should be read as "students with two or more exceptionalities".

**REFERENCES**

Alamer, H.A. (2017). *Exploring the experiences and insights of a twice-exceptional student finishing a college teacher preparation program: A case study* (Doctoral dissertation). ProQuest (Number: 10276156).

Ames, M. E., Coombs, E. M., Duerksen, K. N., Vincent, J. & McMorris, C. A. (2022). Canadian mapping of autism-specific supports for postsecondary students. *Research in Autism Spectrum Disorders*, 90, 101899. DOI:10.1016/j.rasd.2021.101899

Armstrong, S. (2018). *A qualitative study of the experiences that facilitated academic and social success for twice-exceptional students transitioning into higher education* (Doctoral dissertation). ProQuest (Number: 10746626)

Aschaiek, S. (2024). Bridging gaps and building opportunities: How growing recognition of the diverse needs of students on the autism spectrum is fuelling a culture change on campus. *University Affairs*, 28 February. https://archives.universityaffairs.ca/features/feature-article/bridging-gaps-and-building-opportunities/

Baum, S. M. & Olenchak, F. R. (2002). The alphabet children: GT, ADHD, and more. *Exceptionality*, 10(2), 77–91.

Baum, S. M., Schader, R. M. & Hébert, T. P. (2014). Through a different lens: Reflecting on a strengths-based, talent-focused approach for twice-exceptional learners. *Gifted Child Quarterly*, 58(4), 311–327. DOI:10.1177/0016986214547632

Canadian Academy of Health Sciences (CAHS). (2022). *Autism in Canada: Considerations for future public policy development: Weaving together evidence and lived experience*. The Oversight Panel on the Assessment on Autism, CAHS. https://cahs-acss.ca/wp-content/uploads/2022/04/CAHS-Autism-in-Canada-Considerations-for-future-public-policy-development.pdf

Canadian Survey on Disability, 2017 to 2022. (2023). *Statistics Canada – The Daily*, 18 December. https://www150.statcan.gc.ca/n1/daily-quotidien/231201/dq231201b-eng.htm

Coleman, M. R. (2003). The identification of students who are gifted. Arlington, VA: ERIC Clearinghouse on Disabilities and Gifted Education. (ERIC Service Reproduction No. ED480431)

Coombs, E. C., Vincent, J., McMorris, C. A. & Ames, M. E. (2023). Barriers and facilitators to supporting Canadian autistic postsecondary students: Experiences of accessible learning staff and administrators. *Research in Autism Spectrum Disorders, 109*. DOI: 10.1016/j.rasd.2023.102260

Faggella-Luby, M., Gelbar, N., Dukes III, L., Madaus, J., Lalor, A. & Lombardi, A. (2019). Learning strategy instruction for college students with disabilities: A systematic review of the literature. *Journal of Postsecondary Education and Disability, 32*(1), 63–81.

Foley-Nicpon, M. & Teriba, A. (2022). Policy considerations for twice-exceptional students. *Gifted Child Today, 45*(4), 212–219. DOI: 10.1177/10762175221110943

Gilger, J. W. & Olulade, O. A. (2013). What happened to the "superior abilities" in adults with dyslexia and high IQs? A behavioral and neurological illustration. *Roeper Review, 35*, 241–253. DOI: 10.1080/02783193.2013.825365

Harris, P., Mayes, R. D., Vega, D. & Hines, E. M. (2016). Reaching higher: College and career readiness for African American males with learning disabilities. *Journal of African American Males in Education, 7*(1), 52–69.

Hu, S., Kuh, G. D. & Shaoqing, L (2008). The effects of engagement in inquiry-oriented activities on student learning and personal development. *Innovative Higher Education, 33*, 71–81.

Hua, O., Shore, B. M. & Makarova, E. (2014). Inquiry-based instruction within a community of practice for gifted-ADHD college students. *Gifted Education International, 30*(1), 74–86. DOI: 10.1177/0261429412447709

Killean, E. & Hubka, D. (1999). Working towards a coordinated national approach to services, accommodations and policies for post-secondary students with disabilities: Ensuring access to higher education and career training. https://eric.ed.gov/?id=ED441308

Lee, C.-W. & Ritchotte, J. A. (2018). Seeing and supporting twice-exceptional learners. *Educational Forum, 82*(1), 68–84. DOI: 10.1080/00131725.2018.1379580

Lummiss, M. (2018). Self-perceptions of twice-exceptional students: The influence of labels and educational placement on the self-concept of post-secondary gifted/learning disabled students. *Actes du Symposium JEAN-PAUL DIONNE Symposium Proceedings 1*. DOI: 10.18192/jpds-sjpd.v1i0.2177

Madaus, J., Cascio, A., Delgado, J., Gelbar, N., Reis, S. & Taconish, E. (2023). Improving the transition to college for twice-exceptional students with ASD: Perspectives from college service providers. *Career Development and Transition for Exceptional Individuals, 46*(1), 40–51. DOI: 10.1177/21651434221091230

Madaus, J., Gelbar, N., Faggella-Luby, M. N. & Dukes III, L. L. (2024). Ten years after: A systematic review of the literature on postsecondary education and disability from 2013 to 2022. *Frontiers in Education, 9*, 1412903. DOI: 10.3389/feduc.2024.1412903

Madaus, J., Reis, S., Gelbar, N., Delgado, J. & Cascio, A. (2022). Perceptions of factors that facilitate and impede learning among twice-exceptional students with autism spectrum disorder *Neurobiology of Learning and Memory*, 193, 107627. DOI:10.1016/j.nlm.2022.107627

Mann, R. L. (2006). Effective teaching strategies for gifted/learning-disabled students with spatial strengths. *The Journal of Secondary Gifted Education*, 17(2), 112–121.

Mayes, R. D., Hines, E. M., Bibbs, D. L., Rodman, J., Bonner II, F. A. & Goings, R. B. (2019). Counselors and psychologists mentoring gifted Black males with disabilities to foster college and career readiness. *Gifted Child Today*, 42(3), 157–164. DOI:10.1177/1076217519843150

McGuire, J. M., Hall, D. & Litt, A. V. (1991). A field-based study of the direct service needs of college students with learning disabilities. *Journal of College Student Development*, 32, 101–108.

McEachern, A. G. & Bornot, J. (2001). Gifted students with learning disabilities: Implications and strategies for school counselors. *Professional School Counseling*, 5, 34–41.

Michael, R. (2016). The perceived success of tutoring students with learning disabilities: Relations to tutee and tutoring variables. *The Journal of Postsecondary Education and Disability*, 29(4), 349–361. https://eric.ed.gov/?id=EJ1133818

Mohler, E. C. & Godin-Jacques, C. (2023). *State of the schools report: Seeking equitable, attainable, and accessible learning through advocacy efforts*. National Educational Association of Disabled Students [NEADS]. https://disabilityawards.ca/state-of-the-schools-report/

Nachman, B. R., McDermott, C. T. & Cox, B. E. (2022). Autism-specific college support programs: Differences across geography and institutional type. Journal of Autism and Developmental Disorders, 52, 863–870. DOI:10.1007/s10803-021-04958-1

National Center for Education Statistics. (2023). Table 311.10. Number and percentage distribution of students enrolled in postsecondary institutions, by level, disability status, and selected student characteristics: Academic year 2019–20 [Data table]. *Digest of Education Statistics*, 5 December. U.S. Department of Education, Institute of Education Sciences. https://nces.ed.gov/programs/digest/d22/tables/dt22_311.10.asp

Nelson, H., Switalsky, D., Ciesielski, J., Brown, H. M., Ryan, J., Stothers, M., Coombs, E., Crerear, A., Devlin, C., Bendevis, C., Ksiazek, T., Dwyer, P., Hack, C., Connolly, T., Nicholas, D. B. & DiRezze, B. (2023). A scoping review of supports on college university campuses for autistic post-secondary students. *Frontiers in Education*. https://www.frontiersin.org/journals/education/articles/10.3389/feduc.2023.1179865/full

O'Neill, L. N. P., Markward, M. J. & French, J. P. (2012). Predictors of graduation among college students with disabilities. *Journal of Postsecondary Education and Disability*, 25(1), 21–36.

Reis, S., Gelbar, N. & Madaus, J. (2022). Understanding the academic success of academically talented college students with autism spectrum disorders. *Journal of Autism and Developmental Disorders*, 52, 4426–4439. DOI:10.1007/s10803-021-05290-4

Reis, S., Gelbar, N. & Madaus, J. (2023). Pathways to academic success: Specific strength-based teaching and support strategies for twice-exceptional high school students with autism spectrum disorder. *Gifted Education International, 39*(3), 378–400. DOI:10.1177/02614294221124197

Reis, S. M., McGuire, J. M. & Neu, T. W. (2000). Compensation strategies used by high-ability students with learning disabilities who succeed in college. *Gifted Child Quarterly, 44*(2), 123–134.

Reis, S., Neu, T.W. & McGuire, J. M. (1997). Case studies of high-ability students with learning disabilities who have achieved. *Exceptional Children, 63*(4), 463–479.

Rillotta, F. & O'Donovan, M.-A. (2023). Inclusion of people with intellectual disability in university in Australia. Impetus for change. In J. W. Madaus & L. L. Dukes III. (Eds.), *Handbook of higher education and disability: International perspectives* (pp. 229–246). Edward Elgar Publishing.

Rubenstein, L. D., Schelling, N., Wilczynski, S. M. & Hooks, E. N. (2015). Lived experiences of parents of gifted students with autism spectrum disorder: The struggle to find appropriate educational experiences. *Gifted Child Quarterly, 59*(4), 283–298. DOI:10.1177/0016986215592193

Schultz, S. M. (2012). Twice-exceptional students enrolled in Advanced Placement classes. *Gifted Child Quarterly, 56*(3), 119–133. DOI:10.1177/0016986212444605

Snyder, K. H., McClurg, V. M., Wu, J. & McCallum, R. S. (2022). Success of students screened as twice-exceptional as a function of major selection and academic strength. *Journal of College Student Retention: Research, Theory & Practice, 24*(2), 290–315. DOI:10.1177/1521025120915852

Sukhai, M. & Latour, A. (2023). The trainee-mentor relationship in graduate and post-doctoral training in Canada for trainees with disabilities. In J.W. Madaus & L. L. Dukes III (Eds.), *Handbook of higher education and disability: International Perspectives* (pp. 229–246). Edward Elgar Publishing.

Tagtmeyer, C.J. (2018). *Twice-exceptional college students identified as gifted and diagnosed with autism spectrum disorder: A comparative case study* (Doctoral dissertation). ProQuest (Number: 10642726).

Trevisan, D. A., Leach, S., Iarocci, G. & Birmingham, E. (2021). Evaluation of a peer mentorship program for autistic college students. *Autism in Adulthood, 32*(2), 187–194. DOI:10.1089/aut.2019.0087

U.S. Department of Education Office of Special Education Programs (OSEP) & Rehabilitation Services Administration (RSA). (n.d.). NTACT:C | National Technical Assistance Center on Transition. https://transitionta.org/

Willard-Holt, C., Weber, J., Morrison, K. L. & Horgan, J. (2013). Twice-exceptional learners' perspectives on effective learning strategies. *Gifted Child Quarterly, 57*(4), 247–262. DOI:10.1177/0016986213501076

Wellness Services. (2024). Neurodiversity Immersive Campus Experience (NICE). https://ucalgary.ca/wellness-services/services/neurodiversity-support/NICE-days

York University. (2024). York U – A Canadian leader in autism support. YorkU, 3 May. https://www.yorku.ca/yfile/2024/05/03/york-leads-in-building-autism-support/

Conclusion

# Seven

In this book, we aimed to create an interdisciplinary and multi-contextual study on the learning, education and lived experiences of twice-exceptional (2e) students within higher education institutions. Our goal was to highlight both the potential and the risks associated with the diversity of individuals operating at the intersection of giftedness and intellectual, developmental, neurobiological, social/emotional and/or cultural challenges. The individual chapters address various significant aspects of the educational situation of these students, reflecting the challenges and opportunities they face in the academic environment, particularly relevant to its need for adaptation. This structure has allowed for a spiral development of key themes – from analysing precursors, through instructional processes and their effects, to providing recommendations.

We are convinced that the analyses and syntheses included in this book demonstrate that theoretical reflection accompanied by in-depth interdisciplinary thinking can lead to positive change. Chapter 1 introduced the reader to fundamental concepts related to twice-exceptionality, providing the terminology and conceptual foundation necessary for further analysis. Chapter 2 deepened the reflection on identity processes and the psychosocial experiences of 2e individuals in the context of academic functioning. Chapter 3 expanded this perspective by addressing well-being and relationships within the academic environment. In Chapter 4, we demonstrated how migration-related experiences may obscure the abilities and potential of students, placing them in a situation similar to that of twice-exceptionality. Chapter 5 proposed an analytical and interpretive model that can inspire the development of support frameworks in academic practice and educational policy. Chapter 6 focused on institutional practices and presented recommendations for creating supportive academic environments for 2e individuals.

The theoretical and practical model presented in this book enables a deeper understanding of the complexity of 2e individuals' lived experiences in the context of contemporary social conditions. Each student in higher education – regardless of culture, abilities or challenges – must have the opportunity to realize their potential.

More diversity is present in higher education institutions than ever before, implying that instruction should progress from a normative, transmissive model toward an approach that is differentiated to better support individual development, identity formation and positive social relationships. Diversity is a great resource in higher education, promoting more depth in discourse and opportunities to hear viewpoints differing from prior experiences. Taking advantage of this resource and intentionally including 2e students, along with others who may have previously been marginalized, by allowing more flexibility in how they process information and how they best express their learning, can improve the quality of education for all.

Since language shapes reality, a departure from binary thinking in terms of 2e individuals being "healthy vs health disordered" or being characterized by "ability vs disability" or "limitations or problems vs challenges" is necessary for transformation in higher education. This model – the inclusive classroom – represents a spectrum-based approach grounded in a more nuanced, multidimensional recognition of individual needs, potential and challenges. Inclusive classrooms increase the chances of sustained student engagement, support the construction of positive academic identities and strengthen students' autonomy and agency. Such educational spaces would be welcoming, supportive, inclusive and responsive to the multidimensional complexity of diversity. This model can serve as a useful tool in designing support strategies, a framework for interpreting and adapting academic practices and an impetus to rethink the university environment.

The common denominator of the analyses presented in the book is a drive for change and a recognition of the necessity for institutional and systemic reforms. Needed academic and pedagogical adaptations include, among others, additional preparation among academic staff to understand and work with 2e students (as well as others who may prefer to express their learning using alternative formats) and conversations among university faculty regarding inclusive pedagogy. These discussions will help to foster more inclusive attitudes that are open to diversity and willing to respond empathetically to the needs of neurodiverse students.

Collaboration between academics, practitioners and policy-makers is key to ensuring that efforts to improve the quality of academic life are meaningful. In addition to pedagogical change, some university policies need to be re-examined, taking into account the specific ways in which 2e students and other marginalized individuals function – their strengths, challenges and aspirations. Some examples include broadening the admissions process to accept additional forms of evidence of academic preparation; developing a workable system for precise identification of needs and challenges of neurodiverse students within higher education; progression requirements that recognize that some students (including 2e students) may require additional academic terms in order to do their best work; and reduction of other barriers (physical, social and academic) that neurodiverse students experience.

Responsible educational institutions should also invest in implementation research – not only concerning 2e students themselves but also the effectiveness of interventions and support policies, the effects of faculty presentations and workshops, the change in responsiveness of faculty to more inclusive pedagogy, and the results of diversity management strategies. Some important recommendations for research on educational policy changes and pedagogical actions related to 2e students (and others with needs for more personalized education) within higher education institutions include the following:

1. The introduction of a system for early identification of 2e students, using a multidisciplinary process that may include qualitative tools, interviews, environmental observations and/or standardized tests
2. The implementation of mandatory workshops for teachers, professors and academic staff on students with exceptionalities (including 2e students), inclusion and differentiated teaching methods

3. The uptake of individualization in teaching methods and approaches, along with flexible forms of assessment, based on respecting the diverse needs of 2e students
4. The participation of 2e students in decision-making processes and research initiatives
5. The creation of interdisciplinary teams of experts supporting the learning and well-being of 2e students

This book does not constitute a definitive and exhaustive compendium of knowledge related to 2e learners; rather, it is an important contribution to the discourse on these and other marginalized learners. With this in mind, we highlight the need for further in-depth research in the following areas:

1. Evaluation of the effectiveness of support provided to 2e students at all stages of their higher-education journey – from recruitment procedures to career-path support
2. The need for longitudinal studies that explore the role of academic experiences in psychological well-being, the development of academic interests, and both educational success and failure
3. Comparative studies of support systems for 2e students with migration experience
4. Design, improvement and validation of diagnostic tools
5. Attitudes of academic and support staff toward 2e students
6. Participation of 2e students in the co-creation and collaboration on research on the development of 2e individuals in higher education institutions

This book presents an invitation – to further research, to critical reflection on institutional practices and to the implementation of solutions. Successful solutions will enable universities to embrace their role in providing educational experiences that assist and allow more of their students to fulfil their potential. As social complexity increases and the number of students with diverse educational needs continues to grow, the future of higher education will depend on its capacity for adaptation.

We are convinced that the analyses and syntheses included in this book demonstrate that theoretical reflection can be accompanied by educational practice and in-depth interdisciplinary thinking, which together can lead to positive change.

Scientific literature emphasizes the dynamic, relational and multi-dimensional nature of ability and talent, concepts that should not be limited to traditional measures of academic or intellectual success. In many cases, the potential of 2e individuals manifests in non-standard domains – artistic, technical, analytical or social – and may go unnoticed if the learning process does not take into account diverse thinking and expression styles.

In this context, a shift in the language used to talk about diversity in education is also essential. The deficit discourse, prevalent in many classification systems, can lead to unintentional exclusion, even when the intention is support. Rather than speaking about "problems" or "limitations", we should use terms like "challenges" and adopt terminology that describes complexity, functional specificity or non-standard learning profiles. Language shapes reality; thus, its transformation is a precondition for cultural and organizational change within universities.

Responsible educational institutions should also invest in implementation research – not only concerning 2e students themselves but also the effectiveness of interventions, support policies and diversity management strategies. Collaboration between academia, practitioners and policy-makers is key to ensuring that efforts to improve the quality of academic life are meaningful.

We must not forget the ethical dimension. Higher education should be a space where every student – regardless of background, abilities or limitations – has the opportunity to realize their potential. This requires not only structural adaptation but also the building of relationships based on trust, empathy and genuine interest in others. Only in such a climate can education become a meaningful experience, rather than a standard procedure.

From the perspective of institutional development, implementing solutions that are supportive of 2e individuals can contribute to improving the quality of education for all. Personalization, flexibility and attentiveness to context are not only responses to the needs of this group; they are beneficial solutions for the entire academic community. In this way, universities become not only more equitable but also more effective.

**DECLARATIONS: ETHICS APPROVAL**

Ethical principles were carried out in accordance with the Declaration of Helsinki. The project was approved by the Ethics Committee at the University of Silesia in Katowice, Poland (KEUS/O/46/02.25). Participation in the study was anonymous and voluntary.

Author Contribution: Preface, M.G., A. G-M, C.W-H; Chapter 1, M.G. A.G.M; chapter 2, M.B-G.; Chapter 3, D.D.; Chapter 4, E.B.; Chapter 5, E.W.; Chapter 6, C.W-H., Chapter 7, M.G., A.G-M. C.W-H.; project administration, M.G.

# Index

Note: Locators in *italics* and **bold** refer figures and tables respectively.

AA *see* academic achievement (AA)
ability, defined 3, 8
above-average abilities, defined 4–5
Abunasser, F. 20
academic achievement (AA): distribution of respondents by declaration 65; SEN and 63–65
academic expectations: unconscious bias and 45; *see also* Rosenthal effect and academic expectations
acceleration learning 13
accommodations in universities 129–130
adaptive technology 130
ADHD *see* attention deficit hyperactivity disorder (ADHD)
Adult Giftedness Scale (AGS) test 68–70, **69**, 73
advocacy skills 132–133
AGS test *see* Adult Giftedness Scale (AGS) test
AlAli, R. 20
Alamer, H. A. 117
Amanvermez, Y. 87
Ames, M. E. 126
AMI *see* Autism Mentorship Initiative (AMI)
Andrushko, Y. 89
assistive technologies 48
Assouline, S. G. 10
attention deficit hyperactivity disorder (ADHD) 10, 11, 14, 15, 104–105, 116

authentic self 108, 114
autism 112
Autism Mentorship Initiative (AMI) 131
autism spectrum disorders (ASDs) 10, 35, 105

Barber, C. 60
Baum, S. M. 135
Bianco, M. 19
Bildiren, A. 14
Bilewicz, M. 93
Blackwell, D. 90
Borland, J. H. 2
Bornot, J. 117
Bridge the Gap Program at the University of Connecticut 20
Brophy, J. 36
Bunbury, S. 43, 44

Cantat, C. 81
Caruso 17
Castles, S. 79
Cattell 7
challenging courses 118–120
Chang, J. C. 81
Çitil, M. 9
Claiborne, L. B. 44
cognitive/learning strategies 134
communication skills 124–125
compensation strategies: cognitive/learning 134; executive functions 135; metacognition 135; study and

performance 135; technological support 135
Conejeros-Solar, M. L. 72
contemporary mentality and 2e students: authentic self 114; gifted individuals 113–114; human development 102–103; inclusion or invalidation 110–112; risks and consequences of neglecting developmental needs 107–110; *see also* right-thumb mentality
Cramond, B. 3
creativity 5
Crepeau-Hobson, F. 19
cross-cultural educational adaptation 88–89

Das, S. 91
Delahunty, J. 85
developmental models of giftedness 7
diagnostic epidemic 104
Differentiated Model of Giftedness and Talent (Gagné) 6
disabilities: described 108; giftedness and 114; self-disclosing, fear of 126; *see also* disabled students' expectations of academic environment; twice-exceptional (2e) students
disabled students' expectations of academic environment: adaptive technologies 40; faculty attitudes and teaching practices 41; inclusive campus culture 41–42; meeting the needs of 2e students 42–43; structural shortcomings 40–41
disclosure 33, 49
Dolmage, J. T. 32, 41, 44, 46
Donald, W. E. 57
double exceptionalism model 29
Down syndrome 10
dual roles and identity of students with disabilities in higher education 31–32; ASDs 35; challenges 31–36;
disclosure dilemmas 32–33; dismantle stigma 32–33; dyslexia 36; formation of identity 29; hearing disabilities 35–36; inclusive academic environments creation 36; self-identification patterns 33–34; social stigma 32; twice-exceptional challenge 34–36
Dyrda, B. 7
dyslexia 36

early school experiences and labelling 59
Eby, J. W. 13
educational inclusion 50
educational success 83–84, 95; chances and obstacles of achievement 86–90, 96; counter-hegemonic and emancipatory perspectives 84–85; cross-cultural educational adaptation 88–89; first-generation and underprivileged students, research on 85; language competence as critical success factor 87–88; phenomenological perspectives and lived experience 85; refugee and asylum-seeking students, unique challenges of 89–90; stress factors among international students 87; structural and cultural dimensions of academic success 85–86; structural-functional indicators 84
Eide, B. L. 36
Eide, F. 36
Elkind, J. 10
enrichment learning 13
Erisman, W. 81
executive functions 135
Eysenck, H. J. 2

faculties: expectation of students with disabilities from 41; mindsets on educational accessibility 43–45; teaching styles 126; workshops

for faculty and student affairs staff 137–139
faculty mindsets on educational accessibility: non-disclosure, challenge of 44–45; training gaps and misconceptions 43–44; unconscious bias and academic expectations 45
Faggella-Luby, M. 134
family support 61
Feldman, D. H. 2
Fırat, T. 14
foreign students' status in Poland 90–91; adaptation process stages 93–94; cultural space of host country 93; fee 91; housing and employment challenges 91; psychological capital and academic success 94–95; social integration and public opinion on refugees and migrants 91–94
Frances, A. 104
Freebern, G. 59, 62
Freeman, J. 4
funding for universities 131–132

Gagné, F. 6
Gagné model 4, 11
Galatea Effect 30
Gardner, H. 2, 5, 7
Gierczyk, M. K. 7, 47, 109, 110
gifted learning disabled (GLD) 10
giftedness: ability concept perceived by gifted students at university 7–8; cultural and contextual dimensions 3–4; defined 68; definitions 1–8; descriptive and explanatory conceptions 5–6; developmental models 5–7; essentialism 2; formal theories 6; historical perspectives 1–2; identity formation of 2e students 117–118; informal theories 6; objectivism 2; one's own assessment by AGS and KAGS 68–70, **69**; right-thumb mentality 109; talent vs. 4; theoretical frameworks 4–5; traditional notions 2

gifted students: ability concept perceived at university 7–8; challenge 34; Rosenthal effect 39; *see also* giftedness; spheres characterizing gifted students; well-being of 2e students
Gilger, J. W. 118
Gilodi, A. 82
global life satisfaction 70–72
Golem Effect 30
Good, T. 36
Gornik-Durose, M. 103
guidance counsellors 122

Hague Convention 90
handicap 87
Hawking, S. 116
hearing disabilities 35–36
hidden talents 46–47
higher education 97; and 2e students 19–21; changing landscape of disability 30; students with disabilities in 31–36; *see also* dual roles and identity of students with disabilities in higher education; migrant students in higher education
high schools and 2e students' preparation: academic strengths and needs, understanding 120–121; accommodations 123; AP, IB, honours or other challenging academic experiences, accessing 118–120; choosing a major aligned with strengths 121–122; out-of-school experiences 120; parents' role in child's talents and challenges 122; social networks 122; support networks development 122–123; teachers 122–123
Hornby, G. 47
Hua, O. 125, 135

identification issues as inhibitors to success: giftedness 118; negative influences on Black males 118;

neurological examinations of 2e students 117–118
identification of 2e students: barriers 16; conceptual ambiguities 16–18; hidden nature of twice-exceptionality 18; masking effect and 17; recommended approaches 18–19
identity-first language 112
IEP *see* individualized education programme (IEP)
inclusive campus culture 41–42
inclusive classroom 145
inclusive language 111–112
inclusive learning environments 48–49, 51
independent living skills 123–124
independent projects 133–134
individualization learning 13
individualized education programme (IEP) 121
innate vulnerability 82
internships 133–134
invisible incognito student 33

Jackson, D. 57
Jacobson, L. 30

K–12 schools 19
KAGS test *see* Ksiazak Adult Giftedness Scale (KAGS) test
Karaś, U. 93
Keller, H. 116
Kim, J. 87
Kim, N. Y. 85, 86
"King of Tenors" *see* Caruso
Kochaniewicz, A. 91
Ksiazak Adult Giftedness Scale (KAGS) test 68–70, **69**, 73

language 145; competence as educational success factor 87–88; described 111; inclusive 111–112
Lanza, S. T. 89
learning disability 10
Lee, C.-W. 135

library skills 136
Limont, W. 6
Lindeman, M. 33
Lo, C. C. 61
Looney, S. 81
Lummiss, M. 60

Madaus, J. 135, 137
mandatory workshops for all students with 2e 136
Marshak, L. 32, 33, 40–42
Martínez, I. M. 94
masking effect 15–16, 17
Matthews, N. 44
McClurg, V. M. 16
McEachern, A. G. 117
mental health, emotional management and coping skills 125–126
mentoring 130–131
mentoring programmes 48
metacognition 135
migrant students in higher education 78–80; support systems, recommendations for 97–98; twice-exceptional vulnerable group, as 80–83; unique challenges 81–82; vulnerability dimensions 82–83; young adults 96–97; *see also* educational success; foreign students' status in Poland
Mihut, G. 48, 81
Miller, R. 5
Mönks, F. J. 6
Montgomery, D. 46
Moon, S. M. 2, 3
Morin, A. 14
Mueller, C. T. 60
Multifactor Model of Giftedness (Mönks) 6
Munich Model of Giftedness 6

National Technical Assistance Center on Transition (NTACT) (US) 123
Neuberg, S. L. 34
non-disclosure 44–45, 49

normal student 33
NTACT *see* National Technical Assistance Center on Transition (NTACT) (US)

Oertle, K. M. 41, 42
Oh, C. J. 85, 86
Olenchak, F. R. 135
Olulade, O. A. 118
optional workshops: course-related performance strategies 137; motivation 137; study strategies 137
orientation programme by universities 127–128
O'Shea, S. 85
Özkubat, U. 9

parents: expectations 48; role in 2e high school students' preparation 122
peer-mentoring programme 131
peer support programmes 48, 50
Perrone, K. M. 68
personal talent 2
person-first language 112
Peters, D. 59
podcasts 137
Poland *see* foreign students' status in Poland
psychological capital: hope 94–95; optimism 94–95; resilience 94–95; self-efficacy 94
Pygmalion effect 30

Randall, M. 88
Rebelo, D. 81
refugee and asylum-seeking students 89–90
Reider Lewis 14
Reis, S. 12, 117, 121, 129, 134, 135
Renzulli, J. S. 4, 6, 12
right-thumb mentality: and 2e individuals 113–114; diagnostic ambiguity 104; diagnostic epidemic 104; disability 108; and emotional functioning of 2e person 109; giftedness 109; health and well-being of 2e individuals, and 105–107; inclusion or invalidation 110–112; overdiagnosis, and 103–105; reality of 2e individuals and 103; respect vs, 2e to non-2e interactions based on 113; risks and consequences of neglecting developmental needs 107–110; vicious circle associated with 106
Ritchotte, J. A. 135
Ronksley-Pavia, M. 11, 12, 29
Rosenthal effect and academic expectations: negative manifestations and consequences 39; process model of teacher expectations on student outcomes 37; self-determination 39–40; self-fulfilling prophecy 38; students with disabilities, impacts on 37–38; updated process model 37
Rosenthal, R. 30
Rückert, H-W. 81, 82

safety 136
Sandoval-Rodríguez, K. 72
Santinho, C. 81
Schussler, E. E. 85
self-advocacy 132–133, 136
self-destructive behavior 61
self-determination among students with disabilities 39–40
self-efficacy 94
self-fulfilling prophecy concept 38
self-identification patterns 33–34
self-perception of 2e individuals 60
self-talk 137
SEN *see* special educational needs (SEN)
Sen, A. 86
services to be provided by universities 126–127; accommodations 129–130; adaptive technology 130; advice on courseload 129; AMI 131; dedicated contact person 128–129;

disability-specific supports 132; funding 131–132; information about services 127; lower-stimulus spaces 130; mentoring and tutoring (peer or adult) 130–131; orientation programme 127–128; social activities/interest-based clubs 130
Shytle, J. G. 107
Sikora, T. 103
Silverman, L. 68
situational vulnerability 82
Smutny, J. F. 13
social activities/interest-based clubs 130
social marginalization 114
social skills 124
Soria, K. M. 81
special educational needs (SEN): AA and 63–65; distribution of respondents by declaration 64
specific learning disability 10
spheres characterizing gifted students: character sphere 9–10; cognitive 8; emotional 8; motivational 9; physical activity 8; social 9
Stanczak, A. 45
Stebleton, M. 81
Sternberg R. J. 6
strategic support for students with dual exceptionalities: balancing support with independence 49–50; hidden talents, reimaging assessment for 46–47; inclusive learning environments 48–49; intellectual challenge, balancing support with 45–46; training educators 47–48
strategies for universities success: compensation 134–135; independent projects/internships 133–134; self-advocacy 132–133
structural vulnerability 82
students with disabilities 50–51; changing landscape in higher education 30; expectations and unconscious bias impact 30; expectations of academic environment 40–43; faculty mindsets on educational accessibility, influence of 43–45; strategic support for students with dual exceptionalities 45–50; see also dual roles and identity of students with disabilities in higher education; Rosenthal effect and academic expectations
study and performance strategies 135
subjective well-being 70–72
success at university, preparing students with 2e for 116–117, 139–140; challenges in transitioning to university 123–126; high schools 118–123; identification issues as inhibitors 117–118; neurological examinations 117–118; strategies for success 132–135; universities, suggested services to be provided by 126–132; workshops to develop skills 135–139
systemic models of giftedness 7
Szelényi, K. 81

Tagtmeyer, C. J. 117, 118, 135
tailored educational approaches 45–46
talent 4; giftedness vs. 4
Talent Development Pyramid (Tannenbaum) 6
task commitment 5
teachers: attitudes 46; and evaluator training 47; expectations 48; role in 2e high school students' preparation 122–123
technological support tools 135
theories of giftedness: developmental models 7; formal 6; informal 6; systemic models 7; theories of general abilities 6; theories of specific abilities 6–7
Theory of Multiple Intelligences (Gardner) 5, 6

Three-Ring Conception of Giftedness (Renzulli) 4–6
Traczyk, A. 93
transitioning to university: communication skills 124–125; faculty teaching styles 126; independent living skills 123–124; mental health, emotional management and coping skills 125–126; self-disclosing disability, fear of 126; social skills 124
Triarchic Theory of Exceptional Abilities (Sternberg) 6
tutoring programmes 131
twice-exceptionality: categories 11; characteristics 10–13; conceptual models 11–12; definition 10
twice-exceptional (2e) students 144–148; acceleration, enrichment, and individualized learning, supporting students in 13; challenges with identification 16–19; criteria and applications in university admissions **20**; educational approaches for 12–13; facts and myths about 13–15; hidden talents 46–47; and higher education 19–21; masking effect 15–16; meeting the needs of 42–43; parents and teachers expectations 48; research within higher education institutions 146–148; *see also* contemporary mentality and 2e students; giftedness; right-thumb mentality; spheres characterizing gifted students; success at university, preparing students with 2e for; well-being of 2e students

UDL *see* Universal Design for Learning (UDL)
Universal Design for Learning (UDL) 38, 43, 44
universities: ability concept perceived by gifted students 7–8; policies re-examination 146; *see also* services to be provided by universities; success at university, preparing students with 2e for; transitioning to university

Van Dinther, M. 43
Van Hees, V. 35
vigour 95
visible incognito student 33
vulnerable migrants, 2e students as 80; dimensions of vulnerability in migration contexts 82–83; unique challenges 81–82

Weathertone, M. 85
Webb, J. T. 16
well-being: definition by WHO 57; *see also* well-being of 2e students
well-being of 2e students 56–58, 72–73; AA and SEN 63–65, 72–73; challenges of being 2e person and impact 58–62; characteristics of research sample 63; early school experiences and labelling, impact of 59; educational barriers and lack of adequate support 61–62; family support 61; lack of/incorrect diagnosis as 2e 58–59; nominations 66–67; one's own giftedness assessment by AGS and KAGS 68–70, **69,** 73; research project 62–63; respondents as gifted person, perception of 68; right-thumb mentality and health 105–107; self-perception of 2e individuals 60; social and emotional challenges 60–61; subjective well-being and global life satisfaction 70–72, **71**; variation among students **71**
Willard-Holt, C. 34, 39, 43, 45, 135
Wojtyna, E. 109, 110
Woods, J. 33
work habits 136
workshops for faculty and student affairs staff 137–139

workshops to develop skills 135; faculty and student affairs staff, workshops for 137–139; mandatory workshops for students with 2e 136; optional workshops 136–137

World Health Organization (WHO) 57
World Migration Report (2024) 78

Yssel, N. 30, 41, 45
Yuen, M. 61

For Product Safety Concerns and Information please contact our EU representative GPSR@taylorandfrancis.com
Taylor & Francis Verlag GmbH, Kaufingerstraße 24, 80331 München, Germany

www.ingramcontent.com/pod-product-compliance
Lightning Source LLC
Chambersburg PA
CBHW052341230426
43664CB00041B/2601